BUDDHIS

FOR THE UNB

Busy

BUDDHISM
FOR THE UNBELIEVABLY

MESHEL
LAURIE

NERO

Published by Nero,
an imprint of Schwartz Publishing Pty Ltd
Level 1, 221 Drummond Street
Carlton VIC 3053, Australia
enquiries@blackincbooks.com
www.nerobooks.com

National Library of Australia Cataloguing-in-Publication entry (pbk)

Laurie, Meshel, author.
Buddhism for the unbelievably busy / Meshel Laurie.
9781863959599 (paperback)
9781925435788 (ebook)
Buddhist philosophy.
Mind and body—Religious aspects—Buddhism.
Spirit possession—Buddhism.
Self-actualization (Psychology)—Religious aspects—Buddhism.

Cover design by Peter Long
Author photo by Elizabeth Allnutt
Back cover illustration by Silverlane
Text design and typesetting by Marilyn de Castro and Tristan Main

Printed in Australia by McPherson's Printing Group.

FSC
www.fsc.org
MIX
Paper from
responsible sources
FSC® C001695

Contents

I believe that the purpose of life is to be happy.
From the moment of birth, every human being wants
happiness and does not want suffering. Neither social
conditioning nor education nor ideology affect this.
From the very core of our being, we simply desire
contentment. I don't know whether the universe,
with its countless galaxies, stars and planets, has a
deeper meaning or not, but at the very least, it is
clear that we humans who live on this earth face the
task of making a happy life for ourselves. Therefore,
it is important to discover what will bring about the
greatest degree of happiness.

HIS HOLINESS THE 14TH DALAI LAMA –
KALACHAKRA 2017

TUESDAY,

Bloody Tuesday

I'm writing this bit of the book on my phone, in my car out the front of my children's school while I wait to pick them up. This morning I woke up at 4.10 a.m. to go to work, after which I met with my financial adviser to discuss superannuation options. Then I ate a sandwich while driving to visit my father in hospital before coming here. Straight from here I'll take my son to his tutor, and my daughter and I will go grocery shopping before picking him up. Then I'll get both kids home for baths, dinner, homework and various inane arguments before trying to wrestle them into bed by 8.30 p.m.

Far from an anomaly, this was a very average Tuesday for me, and I didn't know how else to perceive this day but as bone-crushingly, soul-destroyingly, back-breakingly, unbelievably busy. Furthermore, I didn't know how I could've made it less so without letting someone down, losing money or putting something off only for it to be a pain in my butt tomorrow.

A woman once asked me, 'What's your hell day? Everyone's got one.' I'd never thought of it that way until she said it. But yes, there was generally one day a week that filled me with dread because a number of immovable obstacles had deposited themselves there.

My hell day was Tuesday. It was the most rigorous day of my week and always seemed to end with me in the foetal position in my bed and my children knowing not to ask me for anything unless it was absolutely life-or-death important. I was always fairly anxious at that point, too, as I wondered how I was going to get through the rest of the week when I was feeling that broken on day two!

One particular Tuesday afternoon, I was exhausted as usual yet charging through the world, anticipating trouble. I was running late to pick up my kids from school because I'd been delayed by a plumber who'd arrived to fix our loo just as I was walking out the door. I'd raced home to meet him after a morning of slogging through repetitive work meetings, attending a hospital appointment with my father, and filling the car with petrol after it choked its way into the servo. Because I was behind schedule, I knew there'd be lots of congestion and no parking spaces anywhere near the school.

I was right, and I was furious. Normally I'd grab a park down the street or even a block away and drive up a few minutes later, when the initial rush had subsided, but that couldn't happen on a Tuesday because my son, Louie, needed to be at his tutor's place by 3.45 p.m.

I decided, with the determination of a five-star general, to pull into a no-parking zone. I didn't feel good about it, but war is hell and pick-up is worse, so I committed to my plan and jumped out of the car to go get my kids. (They were still little and needed to be collected from the classroom.)

Then the lollipop lady decided to get involved in my Hellish Tuesday. This was a mistake. She pointed to the sign and yelled, 'No parking!'

I waved her away and said, 'It's fine!'

'No parking!' she screamed back.

'It's FINE!'

Over and over we went, louder and louder until we both sounded quite demented. The other mums at the gate looked like they'd keel over from stifled ecstasy. 'Who will I tell first?' was written across every one of their beaming faces.

Eventually I lost interest in having the last stupid word, and marched in to get my kids. Moments later, I was dragging them out and yelling, 'Hurry up and get in the car!' while the lollipop lady made a dramatic call on her phone and scowled at me. Obviously she was dobbing me in to a higher authority, but she didn't realise that the plumber's lateness had made me an outlaw long before I'd reached her jurisdiction. This is Hellish Tuesday, lady, and your laws don't apply to me.

I had a flash of enlightenment as it was happening that I was causing myself extra stress, and that perhaps there was another way to handle things. But it wasn't enough for me to do anything about it (though I did resist the urge to give the lollipop lady the finger as I drove away).

My mind now focused on the inevitable and endless obstacles between the school and the tutor's place. I had no choice about negotiating those, but I did choose to sit on the edge of my seat and demand my children be silent and not 'distract' me.

I didn't choose the weather, which was oppressively hot, but I chose to let it get to me, and to feel like it was bearing down through the windscreen just to spite me.

I chose to conduct an inner monologue about how much pressure I lived under and how impossible it would be for anyone else to keep up. We made it just in time and little Louie skipped into his class. His poor sister was stuck with me and the grocery shopping, which depresses and over-whelms me at the best of times, but on Tuesdays there's extra pressure because I need to be back for Louie by 4.30 p.m.

We got the job done, through me constantly imploring Dali to hurry up and put things back, and as I tried to find somewhere to stash my trolley in the crowded car park, I became convinced that the world was designed to thwart mums. I felt victimised by a harsh culture that ignores the day-to-day pressures on women. I felt like even trying to climb on top of the dung pile that was my life was futile, because I'd only sink back down into the stinky middle, weighed down as I was by the many demands on my time. I'd never succeed. I'd never be happy. When we got in the car, I looked at my daughter in the rear-view mirror and wanted to weep for her and her future as a woman. No time, though. Had to get back for Lou.

I started reversing and found myself at the centre of a traffic jam, unable to move anywhere as I was surrounded by drivers staring intently at me, hoping to swing into the space as soon as I invented a way to levitate myself out of it. Losing my temper and dignity for the second time that afternoon, I sat in my car and shouted, 'Well, where do you expect me to go? Where do you expect me to go?!'

After completing a fifteen-point turn, red-faced and fuming, I was finally out of the car space, shaking my head and glowering at the gawking bystanders. Just then a woman pushed her trolley in front of my car. She looked right through my windscreen at me, and smiled.

I don't know what it was about this lady that jolted me. Maybe it was that she looked just like me, only relaxed. She had a couple of kids trailing behind her as she negotiated the crazy car park in the hideous heat, but she seemed happy. 'Oh, snap,' I thought. 'I have to calm down and smile.'

I'm not saying I did it – I was too far gone in that moment for a complete turnaround – but I knew it was something I had to remember to work on. The only difference between that lady and me was that she'd remembered some stuff I hadn't.

She'd remembered that nothing is the end of the world (except the end of the world, which hasn't happened yet despite the best efforts of generations of old men).

She'd remembered that we all have a choice about how we engage with the world around us. Nothing is in and of itself annoying; we just let ourselves get annoyed by things. Sometimes I think the increasing traffic will drive me crazy, but sometimes I hope for a little more traffic – for instance, when I've got a really good podcast to listen to, because the car is the only place I can do that without interruption. When my kids are in the car I have to listen to their favourite music. But sometimes I'm glad of some traffic then, too, because their singing along to inappropriate lyrics they don't understand is so adorable.

That smiling lady remembered to just take the day one step at a time, without carrying stress from earlier moments or projecting stress onto future moments. She was cruising along, not hurrying, although I'm sure she had just as many things to do as I did.

She probably also remembered that everything changes and nothing lasts forever. This Hellish Tuesday, too, shall pass.

What a clever lady.

So, either life is really busy when you're a 21st-century woman, or I'm a complete idiot. Indulge me as I assume the latter isn't true. There are just too many of us walking around like zombies, giving everything we've got and yet still with a terrible nagging suspicion that we're failing to some degree on every level. We can't all be idiots, surely!

As a 21st-century woman, I must be as unnaturally youthful as I am worldly and wise. I must micromanage every aspect of my children's lives while remaining fully responsive to the needs of my employer in an evolving economy. I must be on the property ladder, and in touch with my inner goddess, which means a weekly steaming of my vagina in my tastefully renovated second bathroom. I must be able to spot malware and be completely hairless from the neck down, like one of those cats that always looks cold and distrustful. My nice new car needs constant servicing. It's programmed to explode on the freeway in peak hour if I miss one of its appointments (unlike my first car, a 1972 Cortina that ran forever on bong fumes and Madonna's 'Like A Prayer' cassette). I must be 'off' an entire food group at any given time.

My guilty secret is that I feel like my standard of living is changing for the worse, even though I have so much stuff designed to make life easy and pleasurable. I was feeling less and less confident about how to cope with it all, and guilty because I know that when she was my age, my grandma shared an outside toilet with two neighbouring families. Inside was a big metal tin that was emptied once a week by a guy known far and wide as the 'shit-tin man'. The mere fact that I don't have to live like that should be enough to make me ecstatic!

I've been unbelievably busy for as long as I can remember. I'd always thought that working hard to pursue all my goals would bring me happiness, but you know what? I have to admit that there was just no evidence to back that theory up. Quite the opposite: my unbelievable busyness made me an exhausted, emotional wreck! In fact, I had a terrible suspicion it was actually preventing me from feeling happiness.

And what about the idea that we're unbelievably busy because we're creating a better future for our children? Guess what: we are the first generation in a long time that doesn't assume our kids will have much easier lives than our own, or that they'll fly around with personal jet packs. I find it really sad that we've given up on both of those things.

We assume we're leaving them with an environmental nightmare, economic instability and terrorism as the new normal. In Australia, we fret endlessly about our children never owning their own home, no matter how hard they work, when just a generation ago home ownership was considered a basic rite of passage. My parents managed the first decade of their marriage as mortgage holders on a single and rather modest income, which is just unthinkable today.

So, we're all unbelievably busy, and miserable. And making our children miserable, both now and in the future. Things need to change!

I realised some time ago (not exactly sure when, as I have no short-term memory and I forgot to mark it in my diary) that I wanted the unbelievable busyness to stop. I didn't want to learn to cope with it. I didn't want life hacks for busy mums. I didn't want to find out how other women rule Silicon Valley by giving birth under their desks while conference calling the east coast and outsourcing their bowel movements. Good on them, but I didn't want to know how to do more. I desperately wanted to know how to do less.

Seeing that smiling stranger helped me to realise that the first step towards turning things around was to stop seeing myself as a helpless victim. I had to start thinking intellectually about how I could make my life work better for me. How did I know this? Why, Buddhism, of course!

The first time I ever set foot inside a Buddhist centre, it was to attend a class called 'Dealing with Disturbing Emotions'.

I'd been reading casually about Buddhism for about a decade by that stage, and I assumed I'd get around to practising it properly later in life. You know, when I was one of those rich, retired ladies, swanning around in white trousers, eating good food and exercising regularly – you know, when all my hard work had paid off perfectly. It was going to be part of that wonderful future I was so sure I was creating. By 2006, though, I was in the depths of despair, having lost a job that was important to me. It wasn't part of the plan; in fact, it may have been the first time in my life that my plan seemed to falter in a big way, and it really threw me for a loop. It all seemed very unjust. I felt victimised, and para-doxically infuriated by the fact there was no-one to blame. Like when I bite my own tongue, or watch an entire ad on YouTube when I could've skipped it. It's so annoying when I'm a victim of myself.

Anyway, back in '06 I was forced to face the fact that sometimes life isn't fair, and that just because you work hard and do everything right doesn't mean everything will turn out the way you want it to. Life is just not like that.

I was desperately down in the dumps, and had been for so long that I was really beginning to wonder what was to become of me. Then I came across an ad for the Buddhism class. It said, 'When we are in the grip of a strong emotion like anger, fear, loneliness, or grief, it is so encompassing that we feel overwhelmed and disturbed. It colours our whole being – body, heart, and mind.'

When I read that, I thought, 'Oh my God, that's me!'

I signed up immediately and by the end of the first lesson, I knew Buddhism was about to become a significant part of my life. I was absolutely drowning in negative, destructive emotions, and that class offered a tantalising glimpse into a fascinating explanation for it all. Buddha seemed to think that those feelings were my responsibility. While that might not sound like great news, I was weirdly relieved at the prospect, because it meant I could make those feelings go away, which I wanted more than anything.

This brings me to the single most transformative lesson in Buddhism for me: the idea that emotions can and must be tamed. Acting out of emotion leads to regrettable and thoughtless actions, and those actions lead to further upset and pain. An intellectual perspective allows us to consider the consequences of our actions and is more likely to move things forward in a positive way.

The more I thought about it, the more I realised there was a lot of fear, anger, resentment, jealousy and ego mixed up in my unbelievable busyness. I'd been trying to deal with those emotions through a dedicated program of eating, drinking, shopping and working harder, but that approach clearly wasn't really helping me (or the lollipop lady). It was time to begin the hard work of applying Buddhist principles to my problem. I knew it would be a huge and ongoing challenge, but ultimately I had faith that it would help change me in a fundamentally positive way. I know, because it's happened before.

'So, why don't you just apply Buddhist principles all the time and prevent yourself from getting into a mess in the first place?' I hear you ask. Well, the trouble is, I don't usually know I'm getting myself into a mess until the mess is of the full-blown, sanity-threatening variety. I usually just think I'm livin' my life, man. Goin' with the flow. And then I notice that the flow is going round and round and down the toilet, and taking me with it. That's when I realise that things have changed and it's been a while since I checked in with myself, Buddhist-style.

Change is nothing new, of course. In fact, it's one of Buddha's favourite things! He called it Impermanence, and it's at the centre of his philosophy because if we don't accept it, we'll struggle to operate in the world as it actually is.

Everything and everyone in the universe is changing, all the time. Every mountain is slowly being carved by the elements, and every waterway is very gradually altering its course to the sea. And every person is constantly being shaped by their environment. We're shaped by the culture of the country we live in, the people we surround ourselves with, the books we read, the TV shows and YouTube videos we watch, as well as the lucky breaks and the tragedies that befall us. We are buffed and sculpted by the world around us. That process is known in Buddhism as Dependent Arising.

To explain this concept, the example of the mango tree is often used. If we were to plant two identical mango seeds in the ground in different places – say, one in the fertile soil of Ubud in Bali, and the other on a chilly mountainside in Tibet – we would expect their progress to differ. Presumably, the one in Bali would flourish, and the one in Tibet would struggle to break the surface of the cold, hard ground. But, then again, the one in Bali might be mistreated and die, while the one in Tibet might be cared for like a baby (in a very sophisticated greenhouse!) and thrive.

We never stop arising, so we will always be influenced by the conditions around us. What's more, our conditions overlap with those of the people around us. We contribute to their arising, and they contribute to ours. In this way, everyone and everything on earth is linked, and the way we treat others reverberates and affects many people.

We'll return to Impermanence and Dependent Arising later in the book, but for now it's important to remember that they're the reason we must never get too complacent in our relationships, with other people and with ourselves. We often believe we 'know' people and never bother to check in with them again, to see how different or similar they are now to the person we knew originally. This is how relationships can end in what seems to be a very sudden way to one partner, much to the frustration of the other. This is how parents can find themselves blindsided by revelations about their own children, and friends can find they don't really like each other anymore. Same goes for yourself: if you don't check in every now and then to see how you've changed, you might find yourself yelling for no real reason at a poor, innocent lollipop lady.

Because you've picked up this book, I'm guessing you feel similar to the way I felt: like a tiny helpless cog in the big machine that is modern life, getting smashed in the mechanism, ground down and filed away. You might be thinking that if you don't hang in there, the whole thing will come crashing down, taking you and your family with it. You want to find a way to stop feeling unbelievably busy, and start feeling happier and more fulfilled.

This book will help you do that. In the first part, I'll take you through my journey towards understanding my unbelievable busyness, as well as look at the lives of other busy people and how they managed to apply Buddhist principles to turn their lives around. Each chapter also includes exercises and ideas for self-reflection, so that you can start to think about the unbelievable busyness in your own life, and how you can overcome it.

The second part of the book will take you through some practical solutions to stop being so unbelievably busy and start feeling happier and more fulfilled. Whether you're a workaholic or a stay-at-home mum, single or with kids and aging parents relying on you, this book will help you feel calmer, more in control, and more like the person you want to be.

PART 1

WHY AM I SO

Unbelievably Busy?

So, we've established that we no longer want to be unbelievably busy because it's making us and our families miserable. The question is, if we don't want to be unbelievably busy, what do we want to be? What kind of person do you want to be? His Holiness the 14th Dalai Lama often says that every being on the planet wants to be happy, so I guess the short answer is that we all want to be a happy kind of person. I don't think anyone consciously strives to be unhappy, although it sometimes looks that way from the outside. 'She's not happy unless she's miserable,' my mum used to say about a friend of hers, who at every crossroads seemed to always choose the worst possible option. We all know someone like that, don't we? And we all behave in self-destructive ways ourselves at times.

Happiness means different things to different people, and because what will make us happy is constantly changing, there's no guidebook to follow to get us there. It's trial and error, and sometimes we invest vast amounts of time, energy, money, and blood, sweat and tears into things we think will make us happy only to find ourselves exhausted and decidedly *un*happy at the end. Many of us in the Western world have been raised in a 'more is more' culture in which nothing less than *everything* is necessary for attaining happiness. We feel like we need a 'big life' to be happy, with a big house, a big car, an important job, extravagant overseas holidays, and to be liked by everyone – I'm talking about success, basically, or at least our definition of it. That's why we share memes of smiling people in Third World countries accompanied by pithy messages about 'the simple things'. It's so hard for us to imagine happiness without social and financial success that we treat it like it's a magical secret from the mysterious Far East!

My hypothesis is that we are unbelievably busy because we are **chasing** happiness. Not only that, we are unable to **notice** happiness because we are too busy chasing it. We have developed this harebrained idea that the harder we chase, the happier we'll be, hence the filling up of our lives and the unbelievable busyness.

Further, I believe the harder we chase happiness, the less of it we will ever feel. Pop that in your journal and underline it, or tattoo it on your neck – just remember it as we move forward and I'll prove it to you.

SELF-REFLECTION

Let's jump straight in with a self-reflection exercise. Grab a journal and a pen, and write a list of the qualities you would like to have in your life. What kind of person do you want to be? How do you wish to be in your everyday life? Imagine what your life would look like if you weren't unbelievably busy. How would you feel? What would you rather spend your time doing? Keep these reflections in mind as you read the following chapters. We'll also come back to this list in a later chapter.

1

HI, MY NAME'S MESHEL, AND I'M A

Workaholic

For years I worked the breakfast shift on commercial radio. That meant my alarm went off somewhere around 4 a.m. This sucked for many, many reasons, especially as I got older and had kids. I was thirty and childless when I started; in my mid-forties and a mother, I found it a very different ball game. I had the metabolism of a geriatric sloth, the under-eye bags of Al Pacino, and the social life of a single discarded shoe by the side of a highway. In my mind, I looked like Tony Soprano's mum.

Apart from all that, it was incredibly glamorous.

Even the excitement of meeting famous people wore off.

Imagine yourself looking like Tony Soprano's mum when Hugh Jackman pirouettes into your studio. He does his best to create a moment, because he's a beautiful gentleman, but all you can do is wonder if your breath smells as bad as it tastes.

Having said that, I had such deep-seated attitudes about the importance of work and of having a reputation as a hard worker that it was difficult for me to reasonably judge when enough was enough. To paraphrase will.i.am, I got it from my papa.

My father was a workaholic. I say he *was* a workaholic because a triple heart bypass and type-2 diabetes–induced blindness forced him to retire a few years ago. Unbalanced lifestyle, much? If his health was up to it, he'd still be working every chance he got. He's also one of the world's great happiness chasers.

When I was a kid, he was always looking over someone else's fence – not literally, as he's not really into chatting with neighbours, but metaphorically, always keeping an eye on what other people had and trying to figure out how to get some of it. His covetousness was matched only by his optimism, and the two created many a perfect storm of financial disaster. The scratchie debacle of 1987 was a prime example.

Our town was covered in ads proclaiming the imminent arrival of those cheap little perforated calling cards of Satan – instant scratch lottery cards – and the jingle, 'Scratch me out of here', blasted from every TV and radio in every ad break. My father (covetous and optimistic) and his mate Billie (equally so) saw an opportunity. They decided they'd put everything they had into buying an entire roll of the scratch cards, scratch them all off, and then collect their millions. I suppose in retrospect it's almost charming how much faith they had in the corporation that printed the cards – they really thought that if they just bought enough of them, they'd make a big profit out of the venture. They spent $2000 on the roll and an afternoon at my parents' kitchen table, scratching away with small silver coins. A grand total of $680 was 'won' (meaning $1320 had been lost).

That's the sort of bloke I had as a role model.

My dad never attended any school functions, sporting events or birthday parties. Literally, never. He very rarely attended adult functions with his actual friends, so there was no way we were going to get him to any kind of 'kiddy' do. No, my father was at work. All the time.

'I'm sick of going to everything alone,' my mum used to nag. 'I'm like a widow!' But her complaints were wasted on my dad, who drew nothing but pride from the fact that he was still working while those other blokes were poncing around with their families.

'What sort of bloke puts on a nice pair of jeans to hang out with a bunch of women and kids?' he asked once, completely seriously, as if she'd suggested he dance the cancan in fishnet stockings. God, he hates jeans. As far as he's concerned, jeans are the uniform of soft, sad suburban dads. And polo shirts? Forget about it. He's a worker, he'd proudly boast, and four years after retiring, he still wears 'work' shirts.

Even more troubling for my dad than the sight of a man in a pair of nice jeans hovering over a flash barbecue is the idea of a bloke on a bike with his kids. My father has an irrational disdain for this genre of man. Though Dad's about 80 per cent blind these days, he can still spot a man and three kids in matching helmets from a block away.

'Pfft, isn't that lovely?' he sneers. 'Couldn't he find something a bit more constructive to do with his time, like work?'

When I was really little, my dad rarely came home at all. In those days he was a salesman for an auto parts company. He'd leave our house every Monday morning and drive west into deepest, darkest Queensland, stopping in at every dusty, flyblown dump from Toowoomba to Mt Isa and back again. He'd return after I'd gone to bed on a Friday night. That job was quite literally about chasing sales, and he was very good at it, winning more than one award for his outstanding figures. It was perfect for him because the sky was the limit: it was just down to how far and fast he could travel in those five days and how successfully he could charm other blokes just like him.

Unsurprisingly, my father refers to this period as the happiest of his life. But alas, Mum eventually convinced him to find employment closer to home. He became a taxi driver, which was also perfect because he could set his own work hours, and he set them to ALL. Poor old Mum. I don't think she's ever really won a battle with that man in the 45-odd years she's been knocking around with him.

Like the travelling salesman job, being a taxi driver gave my father the thrill of the chase without ever having to worry about catching anything. He could work as many hours as he wanted, take as many jobs as he could, and make as much money as possible. Once, some truck-driving mates of his gave him a couple of tiny pills that helped him work for three days straight! Bloody brilliant! The comedown must've been a bastard, though, because he never tried them again. He resorted to old-school tricks, like tying his shoe-laces too tightly so the throbbing of his feet would keep him awake. Chase, chase, chase.

There were a couple of key messages about work and being busy that sunk in pretty deep for me:

1. Hard work = loyalty from your fam, no matter how flamboyantly disinterested you are in them and their lives.
2. Hard work = being allowed to be a bit of an arsehole around the house.

On the rare occasion when he did grace us with his presence, usually on a Sunday night, my father never, ever got up from his seat except to go to the toilet, the one thing he couldn't command one of us kids to do for him.

He'd sit at the table and order us to fetch his after-shower shorts (or he'd just sit there in his jocks, if we were real lucky), or to get him a beer from the fridge about every eight minutes, or to change the channel on the tele whenever anything vaguely interesting for kids popped up, or to heat up his dinner, pour him a glass of wine to go with his dinner, clear up the table after his dinner, or anything else he could think of to assert his status over us.

When we'd protest – perhaps because he'd walked right past the fridge on his way back from the toilet and then commanded one of us to come out of our rooms to get him a beer – he'd raise his eyebrows in disbelief, like he was a bit hurt. Mum would then leap into action and yell, 'Your father works a hundred bloody hours a week for you kids. It wouldn't hurt you to be a bit grateful!' The funny thing about Mum is that as much as she complained about my father's workaholism, if anyone else dared mention it she'd turn into a tiger snake.

Even later on, when Dad's Sunday-night mean streak became really well developed, Mum used his hundred hours a week to try to console us and settle the house after he'd turned it upside down and stomped off to bed. 'He doesn't mean it,' she'd say. 'He's so tired.' Occasionally, it was even sadder: 'He was such a lovely dad when you girls were little.'

Looking back, I think my father may have been having his own realisation about the fact that life doesn't always turn out according to plan. He was obviously desperately unhappy, and probably feeling very trapped in a dung pile of a life, like I used to most Tuesdays.

I should point out that my mum worked too. I'm not willing to institute a points system, but I will say that she did every bit of the housework, the cooking, the shopping and the actual hands-on childrearing, while also holding down a variety of part-time jobs. She had no family around to help and no money for child care, either. There was a very clear lesson here, too:

3. Only paid work counts, and whoever is doing most of that wins.

I started working at the shop across the road when I was thirteen, which was and still is illegal, but I knew it made my father proud. One of my duties was selling cigarettes, which didn't seem weird at the time because it was the '80s and I'd been getting them for Mum since I was five.

'I've been buying my own socks and jocks since I was fourteen,' my father used to boast, because that was the age he'd quit school and got his first job. However, his pride at my work record was short-lived. He was genuinely disappointed when I decided to continue on at school after Year 10, and pretty much stopped speaking to me when I went to uni, having made up his mind I was lazy. I've spent the last twenty-five years fixated on proving him wrong.

I know there were other lessons I could've learnt from my upbringing, but every child is a perfect storm of what they observe and how they process it, so this is how that alchemy developed for me: I learnt that the hardest worker has the power.

It's difficult for me to think about work without bringing all of that underlying identity stuff into it, and to consider it intellectually, not emotionally. All of my thoughts and actions are framed by the idea that being a workaholic makes me a good, non-lazy and powerful person.

It's all well and good to blame my father, who I dare say learnt the same lesson from his father, but that didn't really help me change this part of myself. And I really needed to change it because as I've got older, it's become more destructive. I realised that there was an imbalance between how hard I worked and how happy I was. I was no longer able to feel joy just from the fact that I was working. I became so sick of chasing happiness and feeling like I was never quite catching it.

When I was younger and unbelievably busy building my career, my workaholism and commitment to the chase was really handy. It helped me develop a reputation as someone who was reliable, dedicated and willing. The comedy industry is an endurance event, not a sprint, and, without exception, every person I felt threatened by as I worked my way up has dropped by the wayside. They either gave up, or missed opportunities by not being ready. My workaholism meant that I was *always* ready. No matter how tired I was, or how much my personal life was suffering, I was always grateful for more work. Even when I was a receptionist in brothels in the late '90s, I prided myself on being the hardest worker. At one stage I was working in three different brothels and averaging four hours sleep a night. It sucked in a lot of ways, and I coped by relapsing on drugs, but boy, did it make me feel good about myself!

I remember vacuuming the floor of one of the brothels at about 4 a.m., having worked an eighteen-hour day in two different places. My heart was racing from the energy drinks and amphetamines I'd consumed to help me through, which I actually thought was fine until I felt a sudden knee-buckling twinge in my lower back. I fell onto a nearby bed and was worried that I might not be able to get up. Don't freak – the bed was clean and unoccupied at the time. In fact, I was the last person there by that stage, and I seriously thought I might die. Okay, that might have been amphetamine paranoia, but still, I was lucid enough to see it as a wake-up call.

I stopped working in brothels not long after that, which stung because I was so proud of how hard I'd worked. On the upside, I pushed myself back into writing and performing comedy, which led me into breakfast radio and television, with their ample opportunities for superhuman workloads.

I benefited from my workaholism for a while because I was young and energetic, but also because I had a husband who supported my ambition. When we had kids, though, Adrian refused to play the role my mother had played for my father. Annoyingly, Adrian had no interest in treating me like a returning hero after I'd left him for days on end with baby twins. (Adrian and I are no longer together, but there's a whole other book about that – called *Buddhism for Break-ups* – so I won't go into it here.)

I discovered pretty quickly that I wasn't going to get away with swanning in and out like my father had. I tried, God knows. When I realised Adrian wasn't my mum, I hired a beautiful nanny/housekeeper called Erin who took on the role of mother in our household. She cooked and cleaned, and cared for the babies as well as for me. I remember her once trying to hand my baby daughter, Dali, to me, and I just felt really awkward and uncomfortable. I handed her back quickly and went off to find some work to do, just like my father used to.

We probably would've continued like that indefinitely if I hadn't scored my dream job in Melbourne, which meant we had to leave Brisbane and Erin behind.

The move exposed the many deep cracks in our little family, and I'm sad to say that many, if not most, of those cracks led me all the way back to myself.

I realised that workaholism wasn't serving me anymore. It was contributing to my emotional isolation and health problems, and it was making me seem unreachable to my children. 'Are you tired?' they'd ask me when I was being distant or short-tempered. I knew it was their careful, polite way of telling me my behaviour was hurting them. And I knew that saying, 'Yes, I'm tired,' didn't make them feel any more secure.

My father and I didn't really speak for about seventeen years, right up until I had my babies. And then, unbelievably, he and my mum decided to move to Melbourne not long after we did. It blew everyone's mind, because it meant he had to retire. (He was still spending as much time as possible in his taxi, despite his triple bypass, although his diabetes hadn't yet blinded him.)

'Retirement will kill him,' said everyone from his GP to his butcher, but it didn't. In fact, no-one is as surprised as he is that he's really enjoying retirement. He and I can actually have a decent conversation now, although I must admit I still find it a bit awks. He's not the type to apologise or wring his hands about his parenting performance, but he does say now that he feels he 'hid behind being a good provider'. Allow me to translate: 'being a good provider' in my father's speak means providing the money for the happiness chase. He used to tell us when we were kids that we'd all be rich one day because of how hard he worked, and that's why he didn't do holidays or movies or bike rides, etc. He was too busy. Busy chasing happiness.

For the record, my father has spent the last year sitting at his kitchen table watching all six seasons of *The Sopranos* and reading books with names like *Arse-about Aussie Outback Adventures*. And the former workaholic couldn't be happier. I began to wonder what would happen if I tried to internalise his current example with as much dedication as I did his earlier one.

KEY POINTS

- Our early experiences/childhood set us up for how we view unbelievable busyness.

- We associate particular ideas and values with busyness and workaholism, which are difficult to shake off as adults because we've internalised them.

SELF-REFLECTION

Start thinking about the influences in your life that led to your attitudes about unbelievable busyness:

- Who were your role models when it comes to work?

- What values and ideas were instilled in you as a child about employment, success and self-worth?

- Perhaps you are still trying to impress someone, like I was, or maybe you're rebelling against something or someone?

- What activities were seen as important and worthwhile, and what was considered a waste of time? *Why* were they considered important, or pointless?

2

I FETISHISE

Busyness

Even if you wouldn't classify yourself as a workaholic, you might be prepared to confess to fetishising busyness. Fetishes aren't all about toe sucking and rubber undies. To fetishise something is simply to be excessively and irrationally devoted to it. We fetishise cooking shows, smartphones and Kardashians (or is it Hadids now?). We do it all the time, and it affects our lives to varying degrees. I definitely fetishise my busyness.

At the beginning of my journey to understanding my unbelievable busyness, I'd have told you that it was completely out of my control and that I was a victim of it. Now, however, I have to admit I was at least contributing to it, because it served me in a variety of ways.

I picked up the idea of things 'serving' us from an episode of *Oprah* many moons ago. She was talking about being overweight, natch, and she had this guy on who told her that her excessive weight was obviously serving her in some way, or she'd get rid of it. As a curvaceous Kween myself, I found that idea as stupid and rude as Oprah did, but we both hung in there and eventually many light-bulb moments ensued.

This guy's argument was that we subconsciously create issues in our lives to mask deeper ones. Often we're completely unaware of the actual problem, because we're too busy obsessing over the issue we've created to mask it. Yes, he believed that people who are fat (due to non-medical reasons) actually *want* to be fat on some level, and so they keep eating to achieve that goal. He believed that being fat serves us in some way. The trick is to figure out how it's serving us and deal with that.

Well, Oprah and I loved this idea, although neither of us seems to have yet figured out the real reason we're fat (clue: we both love chips). However, I have been able to use the theory to help me with other stuff – like my unbelievable busyness.

As I unpicked it, bit by bit, like Dr Pimple Popper digging what looks like a rancid custard tart out of someone's lower back, I started to notice some benefits to being unbelievably busy. For example, doesn't it feel nice when everyone makes a fuss over how busy you always are? Like all the 'I just don't know how you do it!' conversations with the other school mums, which trigger feelings of hard-working worthiness. Talk about serving me!

And the truth is – like my father before me, who admitted to 'hiding' behind his work – I've used work to get out of a lot of the most exhausting, backbreaking or just plain boring bits of parenting. I've left a lot of that stuff to my ex-husband and our housekeeper, Maria, known as Nagyi (which is Hungarian for 'Nanna'). Nagyi is the heart and soul of our family, but even she needs some downtime occasionally, and when she takes a week off, boy, do I get a crash course in proper parenting. It's so stressful and relentless!

My unbelievable busyness serves me twice here: it gets me out of bathing my children three nights a week, and it also helps me pay Nagyi to do it. Bingo.

The uncomfortable truth is I've never considered time spent running my home and family to be 'productive'. I've always felt like household stuff was what got in the way of proper, paid work, and that it's the kind of busyness that doesn't actually produce anything or move me forward in any way. Of course, that's my father's attitude haunting me, but as a female growing up in the '80s, I was taught by everyone from Cyndi Lauper to Murphy Brown that for women to take care of the home and family was old-fashioned, demeaning and sexist, and that generations of women had allowed their potential to drain down the kitchen sink. As Murphy Brown was my witness, I was not going to be one of those women.

Stay-at-home mums were portrayed in TV and movies as frumpy busybodies, old before their time and with nothing better to do than stick their noses into other people's interesting lives. The cool mums were the ones who had big hair and bigger shoulder pads while pursuing big careers.

In *Who's the Boss?* and *Charles in Charge*, the successful working mums hired men to care for their children; in *The Cosby Show* and *Growing Pains*, the dads worked from home while the mums worked in big corporate offices; and in *Alf*, the children were often left at home with an alien who ate cats. At the time I thought the *Alf* situation was nuts, but now I know the childcare struggle is real for working mums, and I'd be tempted to allow a sleepover on an alien planet if I was seriously stuck for help and the alien promised to text me a photo every couple of hours to prove my kids were still alive.

(Don't worry, stay-at-home mums, I know how insulting and unrealistic this stuff is. I'm not proud of it, but I have to be honest about the warped worldview I developed through my childhood to make a broader point.)

My point is that because of my childhood conditioning and certain ideas about gender, my unbelievable busyness was serving me because it made me feel powerful. Working so hard and investing so much time and energy in my career made me feel productive, strong and in control. But I suspected something was askew when I asked my then five-year-old son for a kiss and he told me flatly, 'I'm sorry, but I'm very busy at the moment. Maybe later.'

Oh dear, where on earth had he picked that up from? Okay, we all know it was from me, and we also know how, when and why. The 'how' was by hearing me say it, the 'when' was all the times he was asking for my attention, and the 'why' was that I'd taught him it's powerful to be busy.

Being the busiest person puts you in control of your relationships. Everyone else must defer to your schedule, which means that by default you are prioritising other things ahead of them. We can't expect to be at the top of someone's list of priorities all the time, but when we feel like there's only time for us once every other thought and activity has been crossed off, that's pretty diminishing.

Sitcom mother–daughter relationships are full of this dynamic. From *Absolutely Fabulous* to *Veep*, we see ambitious, self-centred mums whose first reaction to an overwhelming situation is to send their daughters away, like they're the most dispensable of all the needy hangers-on.

'I'll come back,' says the daughter of US President Selina Meyer in *Veep*, as the Oval Office fills with people vying for her mother's attention. 'You always do,' replies her mother, with unmistakable dread.

I'd like to think I'm a bit more sensitive than that with my own kids, but the truth is that, like Selina, I take my children's presence for granted. I assume they'll wait for me, whereas I probably don't expect others – like work colleagues – to do the same.

I learnt this lesson the hard way from my ex-husband, who grew tired of always being last for my attention. He lost interest in waiting, and by the time I noticed and tried to bathe him in it, he just found it really annoying and couldn't wait for it to stop.

I realised that although in the short-term my unbelievable busyness was serving me by making me feel powerful and getting me out of doing things I didn't want to, long-term it was hurting my kids, and contributed to the breakdown of my marriage. For so many years I'd tried to be the most tireless, reliable, available person in the team, which of course made me the most tired, unreliable, unavailable person in my family. That's not ideal, is it?

FOUR NOBLE TRUTHS

Buddha understood that we humans sometimes act in these self-destructive, harmful ways, and he came up with a philosophy that not only explains this behaviour, but also helps us to overcome it. It's called the Four Noble Truths, and is still the foundation of Buddhism today. Let's look at the first two Noble Truths (we'll look at the last two Noble Truths in Part 2):

1. Existence is suffering.
2. The cause of suffering is *Upadana* (which means desire, grasping, attachment, etc.)

'Existence is suffering' sounds like a pretty miserable worldview, doesn't it? We try so hard to think positively about life, and accepting that it's ultimately and inevitably filled with suffering is pretty demoralising. But Buddha, being the very thorough yet loving human that he was, categorised lots of things as 'suffering' that we might think of as minor irritations or just try to ignore altogether. And he believed there is great value in accepting and studying our suffering. One reason is that suffering unites us: we all experience it, whether rich or poor, young or old. It even unites us with people who lived long before us, as well as with those in the future. The first Noble Truth reminds us that everyone has stuff to deal with, which we should consider when we idealise or demonise others.

The second reason to study our own suffering is that it'll help us get to the bottom of it and thereby ease it. If we don't take a step back and look at it, we're more likely to throw things at it to try to make it go away, but we know that doesn't work. It might hide for a time, but it always comes back. Accepting that existence is suffering encourages us to always be on the lookout for the real feelings that compel us to act out in destructive ways. It helps us see the root of our problems.

The good news is that Buddha knew exactly what causes our suffering! It's *Upadana*, which we'll translate for now as 'grasping'. Buddha said that our constant grasping for things we don't have, or for more of what we do have, is what's behind all of our misery.

We'll look at this concept of *Upadana* in more detail later on. But for now, it's incredibly useful in starting to understand why we are addicted to our unbelievable busyness. When I'm feeling troubled, I'll often ask myself, 'What am I grasping at?' It might take me seconds or it might take me months to figure out what it is, but there is always something I want that I'm not getting. Embarrassingly, I'm often craving some kind of acknowledgement, and the fact that I'm not getting it is keeping me agitated. Workaholism is a great addiction for those of us who crave acknowledgement, because it provides endless opportunities for people to remark upon how hard we work.

The thing for me, then, was to find a way to stop craving those feelings. If I could do that, then my unbelievable busyness would cease to serve me and I'd be able to let it go. Sounds easy when you say it fast.

KEY POINTS

- Sometimes we create problems in order to avoid dealing with deeper, more painful issues. This means that those invented problems are 'serving' us in some way.

- Being unbelievably busy can give you a sense of self-worth.

- Being unbelievably busy also gives you power in your relationships.

- The people who are most likely to be hurt by your unbelievable busyness are those you take for granted, i.e. those who you assume will wait for you to stop being busy (but, of course, you never will, unless you address the real problems underlying your busyness).

- We're unbelievably busy because we're actually grasping at something else.

- We need to study our unbelievable busyness in order to work out what we're really craving.

SELF-REFLECTION

The good news is that by picking up this book, you've taken the first step and acknowledged that your unbelievable busyness is causing you to suffer. You've recognised that it's not making you or your loved ones happy, and that things need to change.

Be honest with yourself about how your unbelievable busyness is serving you. How do you feel when people comment on how busy you are? Have you ever used your busyness to get out of doing something you didn't want to do? How do those closest to you feel about you being so busy? Have they ever hinted that they're hurt by you never having time for them?

3

I'M NEVER
Satisfied

I've spent much of my life focused on what I didn't have. For example, I started obsessing about getting out of my hometown at a very young age. In fact, I can't remember a time when it wasn't on my mind. I grew up in Toowoomba in Queensland, which is an hour-and-a-half drive from Brisbane. We watched Brisbane TV channels, so we were constantly seeing ads for things that we couldn't buy. The worst was the annual campaign around the Royal Agricultural Show, also known as the Ekka. The ads went for weeks, spruiking sample bags, rides, food and endless fun. It was excruciating, because I knew I'd never get to experience it myself. On the odd occasion we did go to Brisbane (which was never for the Ekka), I'd marvel at seeing things in real life that I'd seen on TV, yelling shop names from the back seat as we passed them. 'Oh my God, it's Ray's Tent City!!!' I'd scream, followed by a spirited recital of their TV ad. 'Ray's Tent City, come see what we got, we got clothes and tents and boots, we got the lot . . .'

Years later, after moving to Melbourne, I had a similar reaction when I saw Mark Seymour from Hunters & Collectors and the late great Paul Hester from Crowded House chatting on the street outside a supermarket in St Kilda. I stifled the urge to sing 'Throw Your Arms' or 'Better Be Home Soon' at them, but only just. It was definitely the same feeling I'd had when we drove past Ray's Tent City: a powerful thrill to be part of the world that usually existed in my television, a world that involved fame, fortune and the fulfilment of your desires. Through the looking glass, I guess.

You'd think that appearing regularly on TV, as I do now, would give me orgasmic levels of satisfaction, wouldn't you? Well, of course it doesn't. By the time I'd become a person who lives in the world on the television, I'd almost forgotten it had once been one of my deepest desires. I enjoy it, don't get me wrong, but it doesn't fill me up like I thought it would.

KARMA AND THE HUNGRY GHOST

Classical Buddhism has a very colourful and evocative chapter that I believe sums up my search for satisfaction perfectly. It's called the Hungry Ghost, but to get there, we're going to have to start with Buddha's idea of the six realms of existence. It might sound heavy going but trust me, I'm sure many of you will find this stuff inspirational and insightful. Plus, the Hungry Ghost is a ripping yarn.

This is some deep Buddhism, right here. It's where we leave the philosophical path upon which many Christians are happy to tread, and we move into the ideas that separate the two religions. In order to be a Christian, one must believe that Jesus Christ rose from the dead. That's a dealbreaker. The Buddhist deal-breaker is Karma and cyclic existence, more commonly known as reincarnation.

Buddhism relies heavily on the idea that we live many lifetimes. Whether we're born into fortunate or unfortunate circumstances depends upon our Karma, which is why it's so important for us to create as much good Karma as possible.

Karma belongs in the cause-and-effect basket, along with Dependent Arising. Both concepts are based on the notion that nothing happens in a vacuum, and that everything is caused by something else. Often in life we wonder why good things happen to bad people, and why bad things happen to good people. Buddhism says that the reason is Karma.

This is where a newcomer to the idea of Karma might freak out a bit. It seems a bit victim-blamey, doesn't it? Like it's telling us not to worry about bad things happening to people because they must deserve it somehow. Here's the logic of Karma, though: if I just stand back and do nothing, assuming that the person deserves sorrow, I'm creating bad Karma for myself. Instead, I should try to help them, or at least not make things worse by judging them and their Karma. Perhaps they deserve to have someone help them as they have helped others in the past.

I don't have to try to understand why everything happens. All I have to remember is that another person's Karma is none of my business; only my own Karma is my concern, and the accumulation of good Karma should be my motivation.

Good Karma helps propel me into fortunate rebirths, and I've had an absolute blinder this time around! I've been born human, in a free country, with nice parents who cared for me when I was a child and helped me grow into an adult.

That's the jackpot, really, but it's no cause for arrogance on my part. It might seem like those of us born into lucky lives should feel pretty satisfied with ourselves, as it suggests we've accumulated a lot of good Karma. Well, yes and no. You see, there's a crucial detail about Karma you need to factor in at all times: it runs out. Yes, both good and bad Karma run out.

I'm clearly using up a lot of my good Karma on this life, so it would be wise of me to try to create more whenever possible. Bad Karma runs out too, which is the upside of an unfortunate rebirth. It uses up a lot of our bad Karma and then it's gone for good.

Obviously, given that we live many lives, our Karma becomes quite a mixed bag, so most of our existence is made up of many rewards and punishments of varying degrees of extremity. This is where most people feel tempted to ask me, 'What, so you really believe I could come back as a snail?'

If you're lucky, I think to myself, because there are far worse options.

According to Buddha, there are six realms of existence into which we can be reborn. The human and animal realms are only two of them.

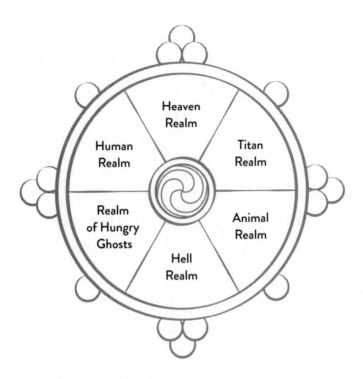

There are three fortunate and three unfortunate realms. In the fortunate column, we have the human, heaven and Titan realms.

The heaven realm is what it sounds like but, unlike the Christian heaven, this one isn't a forever home. Even in heaven our good Karma is being used up, so eventually we have to leave and be reborn into another realm.

According to the sixth-century Chinese Buddhism master Zhiyi, the Titan realm is inhabited by people 'always

desiring to be superior to others, having no patience for infe-
riors and belittling strangers; like a hawk, flying high above
and looking down on others, and yet outwardly displaying
justice, worship, wisdom, and faith'.

I'm sure being in the Titan realm would seem pretty cool
at the time, but it uses up good Karma and accumulates bad
Karma all at once. What a nightmare!

The human realm is potentially the best realm because
we are constantly tested by life, so we rarely get to just
sit back and soak it up like they do in the other positive
realms. We also have the intellectual capacity to improve
ourselves, which our animal friends don't have. That's why
the animal realm is considered an unfortunate one to be
born into. It's very hard to accumulate good Karma if you're
an animal because your instincts for self-preservation are
so strong.

The other two in the unfortunate column are the Hell
realm, which is exactly what it sounds like – full of angry
beings who attack each other constantly and drive away
anyone who cares for them – and the realm of the Hungry
Ghost, which is, in a weird way, my fave.

While Tibetan Buddhism suggests that the other five
realms exist parallel to our own, I believe that all of these

realms are lived out right here on earth. You don't have to look too hard to see people living like Titans, or Heaven- or Hell-dwellers. The one I sometimes think I might be living in is the realm of the Hungry Ghost.

Here's a typically flamboyant and terrifying Japanese illustration of a Hungry Ghost:

You'll notice that this poor fellow has a number of issues to deal with. Most obviously, he has an enormous stomach and a very tiny throat. This means that he is always hungry and will never be satisfied. You can see he is living in agony, as his big belly growls and his tiny throat spasms. (His backside's not looking too flash either!)

Have you ever been hungry and unable to eat? For most of us in the Western world, bouts of real hunger are few and far between, but I'm sure we've all experienced it in some way. The expression 'hangry', an amalgamation of 'hungry' and 'angry', was invented to describe the irritable and irrational behaviour that arises from hunger. Check the handbag of any mother of small children and you'll find some form of snack to ward off hunger-related meltdowns while out and about. It's certainly difficult to remain reasonable when you're starving, no matter how old you are.

So imagine, then, the anxiety and anger our poor old Hungry Ghost lives with, day in and day out, as he tries to satiate his consuming hunger but everything he puts into his mouth jams in that blasted tiny throat. The miniscule morsels of food that slip through just make it worse, as they awaken the stomach for the satisfying feast that's never coming. The Hungry Ghost is in a trance in which he can think of nothing but that which he craves and can't have.

Ringing any bells?

A while ago, I noticed that I'd achieved a goal that had been important to me for many years. I'd worked incredibly hard to achieve it, and dedicated a lot of time and energy towards making it happen. But I only 'noticed' I'd accomplished it some weeks after it had happened, because by that time I was obsessed with a newer, grander goal. I'd lost the opportunity to feel satiated by that earlier hunger. By the time that thing slid down my throat, it was just a morsel, and didn't feel particularly satisfying. That's so sad, isn't it?

I realised that I feel unbelievably busy partly because I don't stop to recognise my achievements and feel fulfilled by them. I always move on to the next thing straightaway. Though never feeling satisfied has propelled me forward, the question has to be asked, towards what am I being propelled? I suspect that constantly focusing on the point just beyond the horizon has robbed me of some pretty spectacular views closer to home.

I was addicted to work, to feeling productive, and got very jumpy when I wasn't working. My ex-husband will tell you that I had to have at least a small amount of 'work' to do on a holiday, otherwise I'd pace and hiss like a caged cat. I've experienced addiction on a number of levels, and I've lived in close quarters with more than one addict, all of which gives me the confidence to diagnose my workaholism.

Addiction is defined as a strong and harmful need to have something, a need over which we can feel powerless.

In his book about addiction, *In the Realm of Hungry Ghosts*, Dr Gabor Maté says, 'It is impossible to understand addiction without asking what relief the addict finds, or hopes to find, in the drug or addictive behaviour.'

Clearly I was seeking some sort of comfort in the greedy pursuit of my goals. The sense of doing *something*, and moving in *some* direction, seemed to comfort me. The trouble is, it's a journey without end.

The antidote to the Hungry Ghost realm begins with recognising we're in it. When we snap ourselves out of the trance, we can start to see what else is going on around us, and where else we might find some respite from our craving. A great place to begin that search is inward.

I've read that we humans often think we're hungry when we're actually dehydrated, tired or cold. Similarly, we sometimes think we need the admiration and respect of other people, when really we need to work on cultivating it within ourselves.

In my fifteen years as a stand-up comedian, I noticed that the job attracts a lot of people looking for validation and love. If you're good enough, you can get it from hundreds of strangers every night of the week, but it never really makes that neediness go away. All the stranger-love in the world isn't going to make up for the fact that you don't love yourself. As the brilliant comedian Maria Bamford says, 'That hole inside you is not a comedy-shaped hole.'

By the time I realised I didn't have a comedy-shaped hole inside me, I'd moved on to trying to fill the hole with something else, but the outcome was always the same: I didn't feel satisfied, and I was wasting time and energy.

As we discovered in the last chapter, we often create problems to mask deeper, more painful issues. Similarly, we often invent goals and distract ourselves with achieving them in order to avoid confronting what we're *really* craving.

These days I'm in a 'stopping to smell the roses' phase. I'm trying to fill up that hole with what's already in my life, like when your mum used to make a casserole from whatever was left in the fridge. Though this approach felt a bit unnatural at first, it's brought up some interesting stuff. As much as I used to turn up my nose at Mum's fridge-emptying casseroles, they were honestly pretty satisfying.

I've actually started a good old-fashioned gratitude journal. I know, how very Oprah 1999 of me, but it's important to think clearly about and acknowledge the things that nourish my life. If I don't take the time to write them down, they just kind of float in and out of my head and they never have the chance to come together in one satisfying serve.

Writing in the journal gives me a few minutes to focus on what I've got going for me: what I've achieved, and what I've just been lucky enough to receive without trying. I also write about chances to practise Buddhism. A recent entry was 'I'm grateful I have been given the opportunity to care for two rescue chickens.'

By looking after the chickens, I can accumulate some good Karma, and they're also very sweet and affectionate. They give my kids and me a quick little daily moment together to enjoy, as we feed them and gather their eggs. Yep, I owe much to those chickens and the ladies who asked me to take them.

KEY POINTS

- Karma is about cause and effect. Everything we do has consequences, even for our future lives.

- Both good and bad Karma run out, so we must keep working to create good Karma.

- Living in the human realm gives us the opportunity to create good Karma, by helping others, learning from our mistakes, and improving ourselves.

- Don't worry about other people's Karma – only focus on creating good Karma for yourself.

- Unbelievable busyness might come from living like the Hungry Ghost, fixating on what we don't have and obsessively trying to satiate our hunger.

- Setting goals and working hard to achieve them is important, but equally so is taking the time to acknowledge your success. Make sure you give yourself a pat on the back!

- If you're living in a trance like the Hungry Ghost – always hungry and never satisfied – stop focusing on your craving, take a step back, and think about the ways in which your life is satisfying as it is now.

SELF-REFLECTION

- Write a list of things you've achieved in your life. What have you worked hard to accomplish? Did you take the time to celebrate when you were successful? When was the last time you felt genuinely satisfied after reaching a goal?

- What are you working towards right now? What are your current goals? Are they really what you want? Will they bring you happiness and fulfilment, or will they just leave you wanting more?

- You guessed it: make a list of things you're grateful for. It could be small things like a sunny day or the existence of Tim Tams, or more important things like your family or your health. Take the time to really think about how your life makes you happy as it is right now.

4

I'M UNBELIEVABLY

Addicted

TO STUFF!

When the father of communism, Karl Marx, declared that 'Religion is the opiate of the masses,' he went on to explain that when people believe there is a great reward awaiting them – like heaven, for example – they are far less likely to fight for better lives here and now. If anything, there's an understanding that the tougher our existence in this life, and the quieter we are about it, the more deserving we are of a great reward down the track.

He argued that religion kept people docile by numbing their pain, like an opiate. Today, our religion is indisputably consumerism.

> Where our ancestors attempted to pray the pain
> away, we try to *pay* the pain away.

My friend Wil Anderson invited me onto his podcast, *Wilosophy*, not long ago. He asked me out of the blue how I was going with my consumerism. It made me laugh really hard because on the drive over to meet him, I'd suddenly thought to myself, *Whatever happened to my Apple Watch?*

About a year earlier, I'd become obsessed with the Apple Watch and its promise to make me move and stand more often. I'm well aware of how pathetic that is, believe me. But I come from peasant stock, on both sides, and my body was designed to prepare for famine. Even though we immigrated to more indulgent shores some time ago, my body seems to think it'll have to return to backbreaking farm labour at some stage, whether it ever gets to eat again or not, so best to store every calorie for a rainy day. Because my life has been devoid of physical exertion since the day I was born, I needed a gizmo on my wrist to tell me I'd been sitting still for too long.

Anyway, I felt like I really needed that watch to be happy. I didn't say it to myself in so many words, but I just couldn't rest until I had one. I set it up and synced it with my other electronics. I conscientiously charged it every night while

I slept, and checked my activity levels constantly through the day. Then I forgot to put it on one morning before work and now I have no idea where it is. It cost me about seven hundred bucks.

I feel ashamed about that watch now. I'm ashamed of spending that much money when there are so many people who could've really used it, and there are so many better ways I could have used it myself. I'm ashamed of falling into a dissociative consumerist fugue state of lust for the stupid watch, especially as I've never worn a watch in my life. In fact, I don't wear jewellery at all because it irritates me, so what made me think I could commit to a watch? Oh man, it's just really embarrassing.

At the time, though, I was supposed to be beginning a brave new life, living apart from my ex-husband for the first time in twenty years. Everyone was telling me I should be joining Tinder and 'getting out there' but I was feeling fat, unattractive and lost, as well as completely overburdened by a new job and not having anyone else in the house to help with the kids during those long hours after school. I felt a lot of pressure to pull myself together, but I really didn't know how or where to start. My obsession with the much-hyped organising and movement-making gadget is starting to make more sense now, isn't it? See what a little critical analysis can do?

Buying the watch made me feel like I was doing *something*, moving in *some* direction, but of course it was an illusion, an opiate that numbed my pain for a short while. It gave me something to focus on and believe in, so I didn't have to focus on my fear and sadness, and could ignore the fact I had no belief in myself.

I wish I could tell you I've completely outgrown opioid consumerism, but I'm currently living for my smart TV. It's huge, it's mounted on my bedroom wall and it's entirely possible it's spying on me, but I don't even care. Sometimes Mamma needs a little consumerist cuddle at the end of a long, hard day. Of course, Mamma needs to work long, hard days to pay for such indulgences. Damn you, critical analysis, don't you have an off switch? Well, no, it doesn't. But once you get into the critical analysis groove, it becomes more instinctive, and that can save you lots of time, money and embarrassment.

In theory, I used to have a long break to look forward to at the end of every year, when my TV and radio shows went off air for about six weeks while Australians enjoyed summer outside. In practice, however, that time usually became filled up with helping other people clear their desks before their own breaks began.

The fact that people like me had suddenly disappeared from the airwaves alerted the rest of the population that another year had almost slipped through their fingers. If you were supposed to have achieved some objective involving me, this was the time you'd flick madly through your notebook to see what you needed me to do so you could close out your year. That might've included a photo shoot, a recorded message, a meeting, a client Christmas party or a hundred other 'little' jobs that somehow took up a full day each to do. By the time I'd added them to all the domestic jobs I'd put off – like getting the car serviced, having a mammogram, or doing all the tasks my father dreamt up for me – I could very easily be halfway through my holidays without having enjoyed a single sleep-in. When you wake for work at 4.10 a.m. five days a week, sleep-ins are the only thing that can restore your faith that your life has some kind of meaning, so weeks of holidays without one was depressing beyond belief.

Then it would be Christmas, of course, with all its attendant preparations and traffic, and before I knew it, it was January and everyone who'd wisely chosen not to blow their annual leave over Christmas would suggest we *all* get back to work a bit earlier, just to get a jump on the new year.

So, I did the only thing I could think of to create some badly needed space in which to pull myself together after a very demanding year: I spent a lot of money on running away for the entire six-week break. I returned on Christmas Eve and left again less than a week later.

I even went to places with terrible wi-fi so I couldn't engage with anything work-related, even in the most minimal way. I made sure I was away until the final minute of the leave to which I was entitled, because I knew someone would attempt to steal the last moments of it from me, which they did. I also knew that they'd attempt to make me feel guilty for refusing, which they did. This was why I had to physically get away.

I can't tell you how liberating it felt to tell people I couldn't help them with their work stuff for a couple of months. No matter their deadline or the importance of their project, after a certain date I was simply unavailable. (I gave them plenty of warning, but of course the end of the year always feels so far away, doesn't it? Until it's directly on top of you, suffocating you with break-up concerts and Christmas drinks.)

Though my approach was extreme and a bit unbalanced, it taught me a valuable lesson about being overly accommodating at work. In most cases, after much huffing and puffing, my colleagues managed to juggle things and either found a way to accommodate my dates or they found someone else. For my part, I had to be okay with the latter, but that was strangely not as hard as I'd thought.

The six-week sabbatical cost me a fortune. I had to board my dogs, hire a car, buy myself a plane ticket, buy my kids plane tickets so they could join me when the school year ended, and pay for accommodation, while at the same time losing money on jobs I'd normally be doing at that time of year. My ledger was definitely unbalanced!

About a week or so into my break, having had more sleep and sunshine than in the previous six months put together, I sat down and drew a circle I'd been tossing around in my mind. It represented the work/treat cycle I suspected was a major driving force in my life.

Basically, it went like this: I work harder than is comfortable, which makes me yearn for treats like holidays, clothes, electronics, etc. These things cost a lot of money, so I have to work harder than is comfortable.

When it comes to dealing with this cycle of imbalance, it's the chicken or the egg, isn't it? Do you tackle the overworking first, or the treating yourself?

I wondered if it was possible to create a life I didn't feel the need to run away from. Could I live in a way that didn't require treats to keep me going? Or would I still spend hours on TripAdvisor, planning my next escape but no longer able to afford it? Would I be content to wander around my house, feeding the chooks and reading with my dog on my lap, in between shorter bursts of working? I imagined quitting my job, selling up and settling the kids and me into a comfy little teepee somewhere. We could grow vegetables, and knit leg-warmers out of our own hair to sell at the local markets. It sounds idyllic, doesn't it? And I'm sure you've had similar fantasies (well, maybe not the bit about knitting legwarmers out of your own hair). But then I thought, surely there's some middle ground between there and here, this place I've put so much work into? There must be something here worth salvaging?

Of course there was, and Buddhism showed me how to find the middle ground.

WHAT ARE YOU REALLY CRAVING?
WHAT ARE YOU COMPENSATING FOR?

I realised that the treat-seeking was just a classic case of good old-fashioned grasping, and, as we know, Buddha had a lot to say about that.

As we discussed earlier, Buddha taught us that our suffering is caused by grasping for things *(Upadana)*. And the first step, as always in Buddhism, is to get to the bottom of our true feelings. We need to figure out what we really want by asking ourselves that important question: 'What am I attached to?' We know that whenever we're feeling troubled, it's because we are craving something we can't get. Whether it's a sandwich or affection from a loved one, our inability to fulfil that craving will niggle away at us until frustration pushes us into action, usually negative action.

So we need to stop ourselves acting out – like buying an Apple Watch, or planning an expensive overseas holiday – by identifying the source of our craving and dealing with it. If it's actually physical hunger that's making you crazy, take the time to eat. If it's a harder craving to satisfy, take the time to look at it seriously and see what can be done. If nothing can be done – say, for example, because someone else is not prepared to give you what you want – face it and confront the reality of it. Your craving is *your* problem and no-one else's. If it's hurting you, no-one can stop it but you.

So, what was really driving my six-week sabbatical? Quite clearly, I was craving more time for myself to do things I wanted to do. I was sick of that always being at the bottom of my priority list. I was craving more relaxed time with my children, so we could connect in a nice, gentle way without the demands of life encroaching on us. I craved time with them that wasn't marred by my own tiredness or by my having to leave to go to work. I craved not being tired all the time. I craved working away quietly at some of my passions, with my dog at my feet, while the kids were at school. I craved having time to spend at my local Buddhist centre, learning from the lovely monks there and helping out around the place.

I realised that this was not an unreasonable list, and no flights or gadgets were needed to achieve anything on it!

As much as I'd love to win the lottery and never have a boss or need to work again (unless it's on a project I find fascinating), that's unlikely to happen. So I started making an effort to do little things for myself that made me feel like I have a life outside of work. Instead of booking flights after a long day, I'd book a movie ticket, just for me, to see one of those grown-up women's films, or have a pedicure on the way home from work.

In Part 2, we'll look in-depth at other ways in which you can create space in your life to deal with what you're really craving, and stop feeling unbelievably busy.

KEY POINTS

- We humans have a tendency to relieve our pain, rather than deal with the source of it.

- In our consumerist society, that pain relief often comes in the form of buying expensive things or indulging in extravagant treats.

- Our unbelievable busyness partly comes from being trapped in a vicious cycle of needing to overwork to pay for treats that compensate for being overworked.

- You could be unbelievably busy because you're being overly accommodating at work. Try to set some boundaries and space for your personal life (within reason) and stick to them. The rest of the world will cope!

SELF-REFLECTION

- Have you ever bought yourself something you didn't really need, in order to feel better? Think back and try to work out what you were really craving at the time.

- Imagine that you've been transported to some magical place where all your normal responsibilities, schedules and commitments don't apply. How would you spend your time? What would you like to do there? Once you've got a list, have a think about ways in which you might be able to incorporate them into your life as it is now.

CASE STUDY:

Jen

'My boss expects me to be available 24/7,
and often emails me at night and on weekends.'

Shortly after stonemasons walked off the job at Melbourne University in 1856, they became the first workers in the world to win the right to an eight-hour day. They didn't just pluck the number eight out of nowhere – it was part of an idea that had been gaining traction for some years: that we humans have a right to some leisure and rest time. The burgeoning international labour movement decided the twenty-four hours in a day should be split evenly: eight hours each for work, sleep and leisure. And so, after millennia of people being worked to death, the eight-hour day was born.

Over the last couple of decades, we've done our very best to throw all of that away. First we decided we must be able to shop on weekends, and not just at the trusty neighbour-hood store, but also in supermarkets and department stores. Then we had to be able to shop at night, and then, before long, twenty-four hours a day. In order for us to do that, some people have to work all night.

In Australia, we used to pay those people a little extra in recognition of their rest and leisure time being encroached on. But now, as our politicians fight to take that extra bit of money away, they say things like, 'There's no such thing as a weekend anymore.' I have a funny feeling that weekends still exist for *them*.

So we started fooling around with the formula, letting a few things slide here and there, just in time for the invention of a new enemy of the people: the smartphone. Our bosses and colleagues can now send work right to our pockets and bedside tables, dragging our minds back to the office at any time of day or night. Wherever we are physically – eating dinner, watching TV with the kids, on a first date – we can be back at work psychologically in a heartbeat. This can contribute to our unbelievable busyness because we feel like we're always trying to do two things at once. We are always working, even while getting on with life's other responsibilities.

The most amazing thing is how rarely people complain about it. I mean, we complain of being unbelievably busy, but for some reason we tend to dismiss the extra hours of work as just being typical of modern employment. Everyone else does it, so we *all* have to do it or risk being left behind.

If your boss called you at 9.45 p.m. on a Tuesday to run some numbers by you, or to ask you to see them about something the next day, you'd be freaked out, wouldn't you? But when they email, we just integrate it into the enormous amount of information we are soaking in from that time-sucking telephone. We might be checking the headlines or scanning Facebook when an email from work slides into the mix. It isn't startling like a phone call would be, and it doesn't feel intrusive. An email is just another activity on another app. We tap it, read it, snarl or chuckle, reply, hit send, and before we know it we're in an email exchange about work that could last a minute or half an hour. This is supposed to be leisure time! Surely it isn't too much to ask to disengage the old brain, eat some leftovers and watch *Ninja Warrior* in my PJs at the end of a long day, without being dragged back into work-mode.

There was a time when we could just refuse to answer the home phone, or screen the calls to avoid after-hours requests.

When my mum felt unbelievably busy, she'd give herself some time off by simply taking the phone off the hook. 'The world will still be there tomorrow,' she'd say, when we'd bombard her with all of our 'what if' questions. She'd also slip her bra off from under her clothes when she'd had enough of life for one day. There was no coming back from that.

We can't just quietly retreat from the world anymore. Do you believe people when they tell you they didn't see your text or get your voicemail? No, me neither. We've left ourselves with nowhere to hide.

JEN

My friend Jen went retro a couple of years ago and made it a rule to turn her phone off when she got home from work. She wouldn't switch it back on again until she was at the train station the next morning. Her family and close friends had her landline number (so retro), so it wasn't about isolating herself but rather about weeding out all the noise and demands of the broader world, just for a couple of hours a day. She did this to try to allow her mind some rest, and so she could get up later, because she realised she was wasting up to half an hour every morning scrolling through the internet while on the toilet. Brave of her to admit, I thought.

Jen is an extremely effective marketing machine. She's a really organised problem-solver and is always on top of her responsibilities. Her boss at this particular firm – we'll call her Annie – was none of those things. Annie had what one of Jen's co-workers hilariously described as 'emotional flatulence'. Feelings just seemed to blurt out of her constantly, taking her by surprise as much as everyone else, and she left a stink of confusion behind her wherever she went.

Annie was indecisive, terminally late and a bit of a fibber, a mixture she managed to convince clients was all just part of her eccentric charm and creative genius. When the clients started to wobble and wonder if she was in fact a bit mad, she'd inevitably pull a sparkly rabbit out of her hat and blow them away with a stunning and successful campaign. From the outside it looked like a kooky but well-oiled machine; from the inside, it was a lot of people running around and pulling things together at the last minute. There were tears and tantrums and drunken apologies when yet another victory had been snatched from the jaws of defeat, but worst of all were the late-night emails.

Invariably they'd be sent from Annie's phone as she whirled around in whatever her after-work world was, and they'd have subject lines like 'Thought starters',

'Mind-mapping' and 'Market disruption'. Upon opening, the recipient would be confronted with a kind of free-association word-vomit that read like someone had cut up a hundred TED Talks and glued them back together while snorting absinthe.

The emails would often end with an over-punctuated demand for acknowledgment, like, 'Thoughts??????'

Everyone would reply even though they all knew that the contents of the email chain were rarely useful, and would probably be forgotten when it was time to really make a pitch or a campaign happen. It was a big charade in which everyone felt they had to prove they were passionate about the job, but there was also the inevitable side email chain in which the staff bitched about Annie, which we all know is a dangerous game. The whole thing required a great deal of concentration and commitment at a time of day when Jen wanted to be winding down. On any given night she could have been on a date, just home from the gym, cleaning up for a rental inspection, wrapping her body around a hot-water bottle to alleviate period pain, texting her besties or just sitting quietly, looking at the wall. It was her time to do whatever she wanted but when the email chain started, her time was over and she needed to sharpen up and get involved. Or did she?

After a year or so of this, Jen conducted an experiment in which she stopped getting involved. She quickly realised nobody had noticed and the switching-the-phone-off rule was born.

Jen felt immediate benefits from instituting the rule, although it was hard to stick to at first. She'd want to grab her phone to Google an actor she recognised but couldn't name, or to flick a quick WhatsApp message to her friends about weekend plans, but she persevered and slowly stopped biting her nails in frustration.

It was all going swimmingly, and Jen was starting to think she'd invented a new sensation that would take the world by storm like *The Secret* or fidget spinners. She thought she'd cracked the code for work-life balance, until she turned her phone on one morning to discover that Annie's emotional flatulence had exploded overnight, and the waft had Jen's name all over it.

Annie had decided at about 9 p.m. the previous night that she hated everything about an upcoming campaign, from the name of it to the font and colour scheme of the already printed posters. She needed her team to dig deep and commence a virtual mind-mapping session immediately. She specifically wanted Jen to kick things off.

Well, Jen of course was blissfully immersed in the latest Netflix original, completely unaware that an increasingly emotional Annie was berating the staff for their lack of commitment, and using Jen as the greatest example of their betrayal.

Jen said later she was surprised her phone hadn't burst into flames. When she turned it on, it was full of emails from Annie demanding she reply, texts from co-workers imploring her to check her emails, and, finally, tearful voice messages in which Annie went through a fairly thorough list of betrayals she'd suffered in her life, with Jen's name added to the end.

Jen got the train into work, dreading the scene she'd encounter when she arrived. Could she lie and say some terrible tragedy had occurred overnight that had kept her from checking her phone? She contemplated throwing it over the footbridge so she could say it had been stolen. Should she turn around and go home, and call in later with a vivid tale of food poisoning and passing out on the bathroom floor?

But before she knew it, Jen was walking through the office and, as all eyes followed her, she went straight in to see Annie.

Annie glared at her, raising an eyebrow and sucking in her cheeks while wiggling her foot aggressively, as though it was all she could do not to launch herself across the desk to tear at Jen's face. Then Jen shocked herself by telling the truth.

She informed Annie that she had decided to leave her work at work, and not to read or reply to work emails outside of work hours. She kind of hoped she might benefit from Annie's unpredictability for once. She fantasised about Annie embracing her as an innovator and an influencer, vowing to make the idea company policy. That didn't happen.

Annie accused Jen of not caring about the business, not being grateful for the job, and not understanding the industry or the tough economic climate. Annie demanded Jen keep her phone on and within reach at all times, or find herself another job. All in all, it was pretty humiliating.

As Jen left Annie's office, she felt her face swelling with embarrassment. She knew she must have been bright red, and that brought tears to her eyes. Her co-workers smiled tightly at her, but she just wanted to crawl under her desk and never come out.

Later, when Jen had a chance to sit by herself to get down to her true feelings, below the embarrassment, she realised that her deepest, realest feeling about Annie was resentment. She also understood that although it was indeed unreasonable of Annie to expect people to drop everything in their private lives at a moment's notice to get back to work, the way Jen had dealt with it wasn't really a solution, but a form of petty revenge.

Ignoring the night-time emails had made Jen feel superior, not only to Annie but also to those who replied. It gave her back some power and control, whereas Annie's emails had made her feel powerless and out of control.

On the flip side, though, ignoring the emails had also filled her with fear. Deep down she'd known she was playing with fire, and when the day of reckoning finally came, her humiliation was compounded by the arrogance with which she'd courted it. It's true that ignoring the emails had helped her feel less unbelievably busy at night, but it wasn't really a solution. It was a defensive action.

Annie had made it very clear that she wasn't going to end the night-time email tradition, which left Jen to contemplate her next step.

It's often said there are three solutions to every problem: accept it, change it, or leave it. If you can't accept it then change it, and if you can't change it then leave it.

When the problem is a person, our options are reduced to two because we cannot change other people. We can accept them or we can leave them, but we cannot change them. They will no doubt change of their own accord, because we are all impermanent, but they might not change in a direction that is any more pleasing to us.

When relationships are toxic and are bringing us turmoil, the only things we can do are change the way we're relating to the situation, or walk away.

It's unreasonable to expect our employer or anyone else to change their ways to make us happier, or our lives more peaceful. Our happiness and peace are our responsibilities. As a Buddhist, it's kind of my duty to suggest that someone in Jen's position try some time-honoured Buddhist tactics, like a daily practice of meditation, intention-setting and mindfulness (we'll discuss these in detail in Part 2). All of these things would help Jen cope with Annie, but I also advocate the third option: leaving.

I know we can't all just quit our jobs when they're getting us down, but sometimes we really can. As we're all living ever-changing, impermanent lives, opportunities for a new job or a career change will roll around for all of us every now and then. In the meantime, though, the most productive thing we can do is ready ourselves for those opportunities.

Tell friends and family you're looking for a change, in case any of them hears of anything appropriate; set up email alerts on job sites; do extra training when it's offered. Keep that gratitude journal going, and write down a clear statement to yourself about how you want your life to look in a year or two. And, most importantly, do the self-reflection exercises in this book to understand your attitudes about work and busyness, and deal with any underlying issues. It's not enough to say, 'I don't want to be unbelievably busy anymore.' You have to be honest with yourself about all the things, both within and outside of work, that make you feel overwhelmed. It would be a shame to go to all the trouble of changing jobs, only to discover you still have the same problem.

By the way, in case you were wondering, my mate Jen found another job about six weeks after the great email disaster. She mentioned in the interview that she was largely unavailable at night due to 'personal commitments', and the interviewer assured her that was totally fine. I reckon that's a pretty cool outcome, because Jen not only escaped from Annie, but also gave herself some control and power in an honest and straightforward way.

5

MAMMA'S GOTTA
Work!

My job wasn't ditch-digging, let's be honest, but it had its ups and downs like any other job. It was actually very rare that Hugh Jackman made a cameo. In the down moments, I'd ask myself why I hadn't found something more rewarding and useful to do. Why wasn't I saving dogs in Bali, like my friend Linda, or working for the Red Cross, like my friend Mike? Why was I still giving away movie tickets and updating the world on Rihanna's movements?

The short answer was money. This was the job that offered me the best living, so the alarm stayed set for as long as they'd pay me to get up early, and Rihanna's movements remained my business. Sorry, Ri, but chasing happiness required cash.

It was depressing getting up so early and being tired all the time. I was living in a confused haze, and I felt unbelievably busy when looking at the shortest of to-do lists. By 6 p.m. on a weeknight even having to empty my own bladder felt like an unfair burden. 'Haven't I done enough?' I'd cry to the big dog beside me, prompting him to roll away, sighing and farting and kicking me in the ribs.

'Oh God,' I'd sob, 'no-one gives a damn how hard I work! You all just take, take, take!'

I need you to know that I was generally the only human in earshot whenever I went the full Norma Desmond. I'd try to hide my hideous midweek malaise when my children were around by lying next to them while they did stuff. Yes, that's right, I'd just find a way to lie next to them. If they were doing their homework, I'd lie with my head on the table, pretending to help them. If they were playing on the floor, I'd lie down and let them use me as a shelf or a ramp or some other stationary object. If they were outside, I'd lie on the ground and pretend to be looking for snails.

Here's the really weird bit: if someone called or emailed in the middle of one of those sad, lying-down-pretending-to-be-alive moments to offer me more work, I was pretty much guaranteed to say yes. Why? Because Mamma's gotta work!

I know, I know, Mamma was already working heaps and complaining very melodramatically about it, but there were two things that made it hard for me to say no. One was workaholism, which we've already discussed, but the other was just straight-up fear. I was afraid that if I turned down a paid gig, even if it offered only a very small amount for a great deal of effort, then at some stage in the future I would find myself short of money.

When it comes to the financial side of life, I felt completely helpless and terrified most of the time, because no-one wants to get themselves into a position where they need to ask for monetary help. Even though I've actually handled my finances pretty well for a long time now, my fear of things falling apart kept me up at night and pushed me to maintain an unbelievably busy work schedule.

Basically, I was kind of obsessed with making hay while the sun shines. It's a pretty common obsession among people who work in the arts, because we know how quickly and randomly we can go from being popular and highly sought-after to yesterday's news.

In 1960, American actor Hugh O'Brian described to a Hollywood gossip columnist what he called the four stages of an actor's life:

1. Who is Hugh O'Brian?
2. Get me Hugh O'Brian.
3. Get me a younger Hugh O'Brian.
4. Who is Hugh O'Brian?

The fact that I'd never heard of Hugh O'Brian proves his point perfectly. And though this is a sad trajectory we performers have always had to face, it's increasingly one with which more and more non-performers can relate.

Technology is making some jobs obsolete. We serve ourselves in supermarkets and the bank. Even industries as vital to daily life as newspapers are in jeopardy. There are a number of driverless passenger trains around the world, and driverless trucks help other machines mine Australia's deserts twenty-four hours a day. Driverless cars governed by apps on our phones are just around the corner, doing away with everyone from taxi and Uber drivers to car-park attendants and parking inspectors.

Already, 'downsizing' and creating 'hubs' is the commercial epidemic of our times. Of course, these fancy terms just mean sacking three people and making one guy in Sydney cover the workload for a third of the cost. Are you hyperventilating yet?

It's scary out there, and the more we try to 'do the right

thing' – work hard, borrow some money, buy a house and have a couple of kids – the more vulnerable we feel. I currently have four other people relying on my ability to continue to pay my mortgage, plus four dogs and four chickens. That's a lot of responsibility on the shoulders of someone who constantly expects to be not just unemployed, but unemploy*able* at any moment. Who is Meshel Laurie indeed?

Another reason I'm unbelievably busy is that I'm a member of the 'sandwich generation', which means that I have both small children and aging parents to care for. Let me tell you, nothing makes you focus more on your old age than watching your parents live through theirs.

People are now living longer, and this has coincided with the aging of the baby boomers, an enormous generation who privatised the planet because they resented their taxes going to anything they didn't need themselves in that very moment, like aged care. Which brings me to the present day, in which my generation must support them through their old age.

Do I sound bitter? Well, I guess I probably am a bit. The baby boomers could buy houses cheaply, enjoyed free education and made free love. I suppose we have free porn nowadays, so it's not all one-way traffic. And I won't again mention the jet packs they never delivered on. I know this is my problem to get over.

I have to say, pound for pound, the baby boomers have been a troublesome bunch, and now they're old and just flatly refusing to die. I expect my generation will be even worse at dying. We have our parents as role models, and we have a medical fraternity that increasingly insists upon viewing death as failure. The miracle anti-aging drug NMN is now being tested on humans with a view to having it on the market by 2020. This stuff promises to reverse the effects of aging by reminding the body how to repair DNA, a trick it forgets as we get older. Consequently, we'll be able to keep living, on and on. Well, those of us who can afford the drugs, which I'm assuming won't be given free to third-world countries as a priority.

So what are we going to do with all these people who won't die? How will we all support ourselves? Australian governments are becoming increasingly nervous about how long people are now relying on the age pension. They encourage us to put more money into our superannuation, to fund our own final years, but few of us will save enough to cover our endless old ages. Especially women, who often take time away from the workforce to bear and raise the taxpayers of tomorrow, and in so doing miss out on years of super. It's all a bit stressful, isn't it? Is it any wonder we can become a bit obsessed with the future and trying to cushion its impact?

The Japanese have come up with a solution to their aging-population problem: they're developing robots to care for the elderly. I don't know about you, but I'd hate to think that's where all my hard work and sacrifice is leading me.

Although, now that I think about it, the robots-for-the-elderly scheme might not be so bad. We could program them to laugh at our jokes, enjoy our favourite TV shows and rub our gnarled old feet, and we wouldn't have to watch them make a mental list of which of our possessions they'll grab first when we go. Actually, that sounds pretty cool ... I'll take a silver one that talks like RuPaul in full sass mode! It'll tell me to 'Sissy that walk!' as it assists me to the commode. Oh, how we'll laugh as we throw shade at the other robots. 'You'd better werk!' we'll tell the toaster, every single morning. Okay, I'm looking forward to it now.

Sorry, got a bit sidetracked there. My point is that we in the sandwich generation are overworked, stressed and unbelievably busy because we're financially responsible not only for our parents and our kids, but also for our own retirement and old age. No wonder we're all a bit obsessed with the future.

Two dear friends of mine sat me down one day to tell me I was working too hard. They put it to me that I constantly pulled out of plans to socialise with them and their families because I was too tired from working, or needed to save my energy for working, or both.

I didn't try to defend myself, because I knew they were absolutely right. I explained to them that my main motivation for focusing so completely on work was to secure a financial future for my kids. That responsibility is mine alone and it weighs heavily on me. (Of course, we now know that there were other underlying reasons for my workaholism, but my kids' financial future was definitely in the forefront of my mind.) But my friends mounted a forceful counterargument that I was over-thinking it, and that my interpretation of financial security was overblown. When I told them my financial goals, I had to admit they had a point. I was trying to make my children young millionaires, but why? What's the point in that? Would that ensure them long, happy lives? No, it wouldn't, but it's a leap in logic that many parents make, isn't it?

We know that money doesn't buy happiness, yet we act as though the more we provide for our children, the happier they'll be, even if the providing keeps us away from them a lot. My son told me constantly that he wanted me to spend more time with him. He didn't hint at it or act out because he didn't know how to express his real feelings; he just came right out and said it, eloquently, determinedly and emotionally. It was pretty hard to ignore. My daughter even suggested we skip our annual holiday, because that was the carrot I'd dangle in front of my kids when they complained about how much I worked.

It took me a few months to come to terms with it, but that conversation with my friends led to me loosening some of the financial screws I'd been tightening around myself for years. The hardest part was dealing with the feeling that I was letting my family down. It felt self-indulgent and lazy, but I must admit it was a relief, and the start of a personal revolution.

It took me back to the question of what kind of person I wanted to be. I no longer wanted to be tired, worried, away from my kids, and future-obsessed.

HONOUR THE FUTURE,
BUT DON'T LIVE IN IT

Buddha believed that worry is nothing more than a symptom of thinking about the future, which is the real problem. He advocated using worry and anxiety as an alarm bell to tell us we're living in the future and ignoring the present. Buddha taught that the present is the only time that really exists. The past is gone and can't be changed, and there's no point in focusing on the future because no matter how hard we try to prepare for it, it'll be affected by things we can't plan for. Like that mountain we talked about before, our future will be shaped by many forces, only some of which will be under our control.

> Worry pretends to be necessary but serves no useful purpose.
>
> ECKHART TOLLE

Of course, living with no regard for the future is equally nuts. This is where the Buddhist teaching of balance and the middle path is vital. It's fundamental to the Buddhist perspective, and an increasingly valuable objective in this extreme world of ours.

A balanced approach to the future entails honouring it, but not attempting to live in it. We need to honour it because the way we treat ourselves, our environment and other people now will have an impact on future generations. What we have to remember, though, is that we can't assume we're creating a perfect future for ourselves, because it will be shaped by literally millions of circumstances beyond our control. Forces as impersonal as the global economy and climate change will contribute, along with very personal things like illness and death. Our children may grow up to be very different people from who we assumed they'd be. I could kill myself making them millionaires, only for them to lose the lot on a hipster quinoa bar before they're thirty. It happens.

American billionaire Warren Buffett will not be leaving all of his money to his children when he dies. He plans to give them 'enough money so that they ... feel they could do anything, but not so much that they could do nothing'.

Isn't that brilliant? I've never been gifted or inherited any money, but I've always felt like I could do anything. Warren's attitude is a great reminder of what we really want for our kids, and how we can help them achieve it. It's their attitudes we need to invest in, and that takes personal engagement in the here and now. It takes patience and commitment, which are hard to muster when you're tired and worried.

I realised I was trying to future-proof my life. On the surface this seems like a reasonable goal when you have the very shelter over your heads to worry about. In fact, it seems like a perfectly responsible reaction to the times and circumstances in which we live. The fact is, though, it's a fear-based reaction, and this fear makes it difficult to figure out where the line is between honouring the future and trying to live in it. What's a reasonable amount of planning, and what's just unhelpful anxiety?

With the help of my friends, I realised I had a very imbalanced and nonsensical view of the benefits my unbelievable busyness would have for my future self and my children. I'd become increasingly obsessed with building a safety net around my family, but I had to be reminded that it's impossible to know what threats will come our way, let alone what shape that net will need to be. The one investment that seems to deliver a high return is time. Only by being present can we forge strong relationships, and surely they are the most reliable safety nets of all.

One of my father's favourite sayings is 'Hindsight is a beautiful thing,' although I don't think he really sees it as 'beautiful' because he usually says it when reminiscing about some lost opportunity he believes would have changed everything for him. He talks about houses he sold and wishes he hadn't, businesses he wishes he'd bought and didn't, and the workaholism that made sense to him as a younger man because he thought it was guaranteeing all of us a certain type of future. Eerie, isn't it?

The inescapable truth is that for all their hard work, my parents did not end up rich. They won't be leaving a pile of money for their children, as was their intention. They live in a granny flat in my backyard on the aforementioned age pension. They did everything right their entire lives, and planned and strategised with as much commitment as anyone. Life happens, no matter how much you try to control it. Though my parents' living situation is far from unfortunate, it's far from what they planned, which is a lesson for us all.

KEY POINTS

- Fears about job security, a lack of money or self-funding your retirement could mean you're overworking, contributing to your unbelievable busyness.

- This is compounded by our changing economy and the fact that technology is making some jobs obsolete.

- It's difficult to let go of our busyness when we've got people depending on us for financial and material security.

- Don't be afraid to be honest with your friends about your unbelievable busyness. They might be able to help you gain some perspective on what's really driving it.

- Money doesn't equal happiness. It's more important that you spend time with your loved ones and build your relationship with them.

- Anxiety and worry are often signs that we're trying to live in the future, at the expense of the present.

- We can't control the future, so we need to find a way to honour it without trying to live in it.

SELF-REFLECTION

- Take some time to think about how much you are sacrificing for your imagined future. How many social and family engagements, or just fun little moments, do you miss out on because you're working towards this future fantasy?

- Think clearly about your financial goals for your family. Are you trying to make them rich? Why? No, really, *why*? Though it might seem like a great goal, when we think about it more deeply it's not certain that money will ensure long, happy lives for our children. What kind of people do you think your sacrifices will make them?

CASE STUDY:

Nikki

'I have no control over my unbelievable busyness –
there are too many people depending on me.'

As a nurse, Nikki felt a wonderful confidence about handling things other people fear and cringe at. It was hard and heavy work, but she knew that sometimes she was the only ray of sunshine in sick people's lives, and that made it all worthwhile. She was quite famous around the hospital for her ability to engage with lots of different kinds of people. She could be cheeky and raucous with a patient in one room, then walk next door and be very gentle and quietly spoken with another. Both patients would feel comforted by her and would ask after her constantly when she wasn't on shift.

Nikki coped so well with the job because she never let it overwhelm her. She was very good at compartmentalising her life. When she was at work, she was fully focused on work, but when she wasn't at work, she thought very little about it. If it ever started getting to her, Nikki wasn't too proud to take advantage of the free counselling sessions offered to the hospital staff. She had a close and happy family, lots of friends and a fun social life. People often told her she'd 'cracked the code' of work-life balance.

Then, when Nikki was three months pregnant with her first child, her mum Jan was diagnosed with breast cancer. It was assumed that Nikki, as a medical expert and the eldest child, would attend every appointment with her mum, coordinate her care and report back to the rest of her family. Before Nikki went on maternity leave at thirty-four weeks, she'd been waddling into the hospital every single day, either to work or to sit with her mum while she underwent chemo, had a scan, or received results.

In the evenings, Nikki washed and folded tiny singlets or constructed flat-pack nursery furniture while talking to her siblings on the phone, explaining their mum's results and the likely next steps, and encouraging them when they felt frightened and overwhelmed.

Nikki's partner, Celia, started to get a little resentful of the responsibility Nikki was shouldering. She and Nikki had planned this pre-baby period meticulously, with lots of downtime together and even a babymoon in Bali, but all of that went out the window as Nikki's mum's cancer fight intensified. When their son was born, even the peaceful homebirth they'd talked about for years never eventuated, as Nikki's blood pressure soared and she was forced to have an emergency caesarian.

Celia blamed Nikki's family for the pregnancy complications, and tensions remained high when the baby came home. Nikki's mum sensed the tension and felt guilty, Nikki's dad and siblings thought Celia was being a bitch, and the baby had colic and screamed twenty-four hours a day.

Nikki's life had been busy before, but as the mother of a colicky newborn, the daughter of a cancer patient and the partner of a resentful wife, she felt like she was living under a weight of unbelievable busyness that threatened to squash her flat. Nikki was frantically trying to live up to her responsibilities and soothe everyone's frazzled nerves. She was now lugging the little one to her mum's appointments, hiding in corners with a nappy draped over her shoulder to feed him, because neither she nor her father wanted him to see her bare boob. She walked the hallways, rhythmically rocking the pram to try to get the baby to sleep while texting her siblings and her wife endlessly. She seemed to be stuck in traffic or waiting at the chemist at least once a day, praying both her baby and her bladder could hold on just a little longer.

Nikki had no idea how to alleviate some of the crushing pressure without letting down someone she loved. She didn't even have anyone to complain to – Celia, her normal sounding board, would go right off about the family at the slightest provocation. Inevitably it ended in an argument in which Nikki vigorously defended her family, even though she was also getting pretty sick of them, and Celia blamed them for everything from the baby's lack of routine to her own weight gain. Nikki knew they were both taking extreme and often ridiculous positions in these arguments, but she couldn't quite bring herself to admit it in the heat of the battle. She and Celia had never fought like this before and it scared her.

She thought that going to her mother about her problems would just be rude and insensitive, and her siblings had made it clear in a hundred different ways that they were not up for any more problems, and certainly not from their rock, Nikki. As for the hospital counsellor or her friends, Nikki felt exhausted just thinking about fitting in a visit.

She could barely commit to showering every day – how on earth was she going to find the time and energy to talk to someone about the complicated truth of her life? She felt like her world had no boundaries, and she blamed herself and her inability to whip herself and her baby into a perfect, predictable daily routine. The harder she tried to create this routine, the more she felt like a failure.

Nikki was dealing with a lot of new and unwelcome sensations and feelings. Her identity and ego were dependent on her being everyone's favourite incredible coping machine. She knew for sure she wasn't that person anymore, so who was she? Was she still likeable and valuable? Would her friends still admire her now that she wasn't living a perfectly balanced life? Would Celia want to stay with her if she wasn't the partner she'd been before? Could she ever like herself again?

It's all very dramatic, isn't it? But let's remember the lack of sleep involved!

Nikki had never before experienced this crushing sense of failure, of not being able to cope. Her fear of falling in a heap was so foreign that she even struggled to identify it, and it was easy for her and everyone else in her life to dismiss the dimming of her personality as 'baby blues'.

Becoming a parent is an incredibly intense and life-changing experience, as is facing our parents' mortality. To have both of these events coincide is a phenomenally powerful turn of events. Of course Nikki had been changed by them. But she needn't have worried – as we know, change is completely normal and inevitable. It didn't mean that she'd never feel great again – in fact, quite the opposite.

Both of these events are bound to trigger childhood hurts and worries. When I was a child, I had a recurring nightmare in which my mother would suddenly disappear from her seat behind the wheel of our car as it kept moving down the main street of our town. It was terrifying, confusing and hurtful because we have such a primal attachment to our mums and fear of losing them. Becoming that person for another little human is an enormous responsibility that few of us ever feel worthy of. It makes us realise that our own mothers were not the all-knowing experts we thought they were when we were little. They were just like us, tentatively making it up as they went along, trying to look confident and lying a lot. That's a weird realisation. It's a bit like finding out there is no wizard behind the curtain. That's when we're forced to accept that we're never going to grow into an all-knowing, expert wizard either, which I for one was counting on. I remember looking down at my babies and thinking, *Oh no, I'm still me!*

Becoming a parent and potentially losing a parent both change the way we see ourselves and are seen by other people, whether we are ready to accept that or not. As the eldest child in her family, once she became a parent Nikki was perceived by her younger siblings as more of a grown-up than ever. They didn't offer her solace or practical help, instead they leant on her more heavily for those things.

For her part, Celia felt that the fact that they were now a little family unit of their own meant that Nikki should prioritise them above everyone else. Celia made it clear she felt disappointed in Nikki's performance as a partner and mother. Is there anything worse than that?

While googling during a 2 a.m. feed one night, Nikki came across an interesting article about the 'Everything's Great Game'. You know that game where we tell people everything's great when it's not? Yeah, that one.

Anyone who saw what was going on in her life had to know that things were pretty tough for Nikki, yet she kept telling everyone that everything was great, and they kept letting her get away with saying it. Very few people have the guts to confront us in the Everything's Great Game, because they know it's fraught with danger. Sometimes when our friends and family refuse to play along, we cut them out of our lives because the game feels like the only thing holding us together. To be challenged when we tell people we're great is very hard on the ego. It's embarrassing.

The article advised players to break the rules by telling someone what they were really feeling. It instructed players to choose the listener carefully, so as not to end up consoling someone else. It may come as no surprise to you that the best players of the Everything's Great Game are usually very focused on caring for others. Having the time and energy for generosity creates the impression that we are so completely on top of our own lives that we have resources left over to help others. Sometimes we do, but sometimes we pretend to, out of ego – because we want to be admired – and fear, because we're scared of what others will think if they know our true feelings.

Nikki chose to confide in her lovely neighbour Trish, a calm straight shooter who, as the mother of twenty-somethings, Nikki guessed would have both empathy and practical tips in abundance. Trish was also next door, which meant Nikki wouldn't have to put on a clean bra or drive anywhere, both very big ticks in the Trish column.

Another big tick was Trish's emotional distance from Nikki's life. She knew enough not to need her whole life story, but she was also impartial enough that she wouldn't be hurt by anything Nikki said. There's nothing worse than editing your story of woe so as to spare the feelings of the listener, is there? It's so much better to find someone with nothing to win or lose from your honesty, someone who won't make it all about themselves.

While the baby slept in the pram one afternoon, Nikki left the washing and sterilising and took up Trish's offer of a coffee and a chat.

Of course the floodgates opened, and of course she felt embarrassed and awkward as hell. But after blurting it all out and eating a couple of nice biscuits, Nikki felt lighter for having said it to someone who listened without judgement.

Trish didn't flinch when Nikki cried. She simply grabbed the box of tissues from the top of the fridge and flicked the kettle back on. Trish didn't gasp when Nikki said she sometimes fantasised about running away and not even taking the baby. Trish didn't raise an eyebrow when Nikki said she felt let down by her parents when they went on holiday, because if her mum was well enough to travel, she was probably well enough to look after the baby for a night, which she'd never offered to do.

That last one was Nikki's most shameful secret. She sometimes felt mad at her mum for being too sick to rescue her from the baby. 'Even an afternoon would help,' she sniffled, and then the tears flowed again as she blurted, 'I'm just so tired!'

Because Trish didn't know her that well, Nikki didn't feel the need to be her 'old' self. She was able to relax and be herself rather than putting lots of energy into a facade.

This overwhelmed, snotty mess of a woman was the real Nikki in that moment.

It took an enormous amount of courage to allow Trish to see her like that, but the benefit was that Trish was able to engage with the real Nikki and offer real comfort, support and advice.

Trish recounted stories of low moments from her own time as a young mum, not to make it all about her but to reassure Nikki it was natural, normal and pretty much inevitable, and also impermanent. Yes, it felt like a terrifying new world order, but actually it was a short, intense period in what would no doubt be a long life full of many ups and downs.

Nikki had been scared by the intense escalation of her downward spiral because she didn't know where it would end, and she'd worried about never getting her old life back. Trish was able to tell her, with some authority, that the baby-fog would lift, the colic would abate, Celia's territorial grumpiness sounded pretty natural and, no, she'd never get her old life back, but there was no reason her new life couldn't be better.

On a practical note, Trish offered to babysit a couple of afternoons a week, which felt to Nikki like the most generous gift she'd ever been given. There was one condition, though: Trish insisted that Nikki spend at least one of those afternoons quietly alone, either sleeping or relaxing in some way. She was not to give that time away to anyone else. In fact, Trish suggested she didn't tell anyone about the arrangement, so no-one would see it as an opportunity to ask Nikki to help them.

Nikki's first afternoon alone was pretty overwhelming. With four hours to herself, she didn't know whether to laugh or cry. In the end, she slept and showered. Luxury!

Everything improved from that first nap. Being cared for was what really lifted Nikki's spirits. It was somewhat hard to accept at first, as she'd always been the caregiver and she believed it was what people valued most about her. She asked Trish again and again if she didn't mind taking the baby, and Trish assured her that not only was it fine, it was lovely to have someone to care for now that her kids had left the nest. Nikki was being valued for letting someone care for her and her baby. It did her head in but she was too grateful to fight it. She felt herself growing from the experience, and seeing a different side of herself.

She started talking to Celia about her feelings again, and asked for help. To her surprise, Celia was thrilled. She confessed to having felt a bit left out, as by the time she'd get home from work, Nikki was often too worn out to tell her what had happened with the baby during the day. Celia wanted to be useful and care for her family, so she asked Nikki's permission to speak to her siblings, and before the night was out, there was a new roster system in place for their mum's treatment.

Nikki decided not to ask Celia what she'd told her family. She was used to them thinking of her as bulletproof, and Celia must have at least hinted that she was struggling, which was hard on Nikki's ego. But she had to trust Celia, her partner who loved her, to help her. She had to surrender.

Each sibling texted her to thank her for all she'd done,

and to insist she take it easy for a while. It was a growth experience for them too, with her youngest brother in particular using the opportunity to step up and change the way he was viewed in the family. He confided later that he developed a newfound confidence from being more involved in supporting his parents.

It wasn't all smooth sailing. Nikki's mum felt guilty, because that's what mums do. She kept asking if Nikki was mad at her, which of course is a question that can only have one answer, regardless of the truth, and no matter what Nikki said, her mum didn't believe her. Nikki's dad was angry that his sick wife felt guilty and burdensome, because that's what dads do, and he stopped talking to Nikki altogether for a while, which was awkward and made Nikki feel like an insecure child.

She expressed her feelings, not only to Celia but also to her siblings, who empathised completely, knowing what it was like to receive their dad's cold shoulder. They jumped right in to smooth things over.

For the first time in her life, Nikki's siblings were taking care of her and it felt really nice. The more she allowed people to care for her, the more comfortable she felt letting them see her as imperfect and even vulnerable.

Over time, Nikki stopped yearning for her old life. Her new life was certainly more complicated, but it was also richer, and when she eventually went back to work (part-time), she felt a deeper understanding and compassion for the families of her patients. When her mother passed away, Nikki and her siblings were equal partners in their grief. Each of them had spent a lot of time with their mum, developing their relationship with her and nursing her gently through her final days, just as she'd nursed them through their first.

The siblings had strengthened their relationships with each other, too. They'd previously relied on their mum to act as a conduit between them, sharing their news and getting them together once or twice a year. By the time she died, they were genuinely and deeply engaged with each other's lives – exactly what every mother wants. For their father's part, he'd had to accept his children as adults and equals. He'd had to accept their help too, which was hard on the old boy but Nikki, having had some experience with accepting help against her instincts, worked compassionately with him on doing the same.

6

I'M

Disturbed and Deluded,

AND SO ARE YOU

I had a terrible habit of being preoccupied by things I was worried might happen, and by things that had happened that I regretted. Both of these scenarios added to my feeling unbelievably busy. For one thing, they often prevented me from sleeping, which made everything harder the next day. They affected my concentration and sometimes led to me making mistakes and needing to repeat tasks. Most importantly, though, they would cause me to succumb to disturbing emotions that encouraged me to see and engage with the world in a negative light, creating time- and energy-consuming drama.

The *Great Tibetan Dictionary* (*bod kyi tshig mdzod chen mo*) defines disturbing emotions as 'mental events that incite one to unvirtuous actions and cause one's being to be very [unpeaceful]'.

We've all acted irrationally when we've felt stressed and exhausted, only to come to our senses later and wonder when we developed the ability to turn into The Hulk. As the ad for my first ever Buddhist class said, 'When we are in the grip of a strong emotion like anger, fear, loneliness, or grief, it is so encompassing that we feel overwhelmed and disturbed. It colours our whole being – body, heart, and mind.'

The problem with disturbing emotions is they fling right back and hurt us, in so many ways. Remember how I abused the lollipop lady? It created bad Karma for myself and stressed my kids out, which planted a seed of anxiety in their growing personalities and negatively affected their arising. I embarrassed myself in front of the other school mums, who I have to see constantly, as well as all the randoms in the shopping centre car park. When you engage with the world from a place of anger, fear, hatred, etc., you're actually creating angry, fearful, hateful experiences for yourself. It reminds me of something wonderful that Wil Anderson said when we podcasted together recently: 'There should be two horns in cars, one that beeps like normal and one that says, "I'm not really angry at you, it's something else!"'

Road rage is such a great example of the kind of horrible circumstances that can arise from entering a situation with disturbing emotions. When it comes to traffic fury, we're usually disturbed by angry tiredness, built-up frustration from work and/or fear of running late. And we act out in ways that sometimes frighten others, and sometimes get us punched in the face, depending on how we choose our victims.

Let's go back to my favourite Buddhist lesson for a moment:

> Acting out of emotion leads to regrettable and thoughtless actions, and those actions lead to further upset and pain. An intellectual perspective allows us to consider the consequences of our actions and is more likely to move things forward in a positive way.

The disturbing emotions that relate most to my extreme busyness are fear, jealousy, and pride.

As discussed earlier, I was fearful of ending up unemployed and irrelevant in my industry, not to mention broke.

I was jealous of people whom I thought were more successful than me and getting more creatively fulfilling opportunities. I was also too proud to admit I couldn't work this hard anymore. Those were the powerful forces that kept me moving wearily forward day in and day out. They were why my unhappiness didn't seem like a good enough reason to change my work habits. I was more focused on finding ways to ignore those feelings than on committing to making the changes necessary for a different life, because my self-worth was so dependent on my work life.

When we link our self-worth too closely to our work life, we hand it over to other people. Our morals can become easily compromised under these circumstances because we become more invested in how other people see us than in how we see ourselves. It's not too big a leap from here to a place in which we might throw someone under the proverbial bus in order to make ourselves look better to our superiors, or claim an idea as our own that originated elsewhere. What follows next can be a heavy internal battle between the part of us that knows these kinds of actions are wrong, and the part of us that craves the validation of others.

Yup, that's right – we're back to craving! Gosh that Buddha was a smart bloke. He knew that we feel disturbing emotions because we're really craving something deeper, trickier and more vulnerable. In a way, those disturbing emotions protect our true feelings because they cause us to act out and create other problems that distract us from the *real* problem, so we never have to deal with it. All of this, of course, leads to us feeling unbelievably busy as we waste time and energy on diversions and distractions that prevent us from getting to the heart of things.

There's probably a bit of future-thinking involved, too, when we place all our self-worth in work. We might console ourselves with the idea that it will all be worth it when we get that promotion, or that we'll treat people well when we're running things – we just have to make a few sacrifices to get there first. *If you want to make an omelette*, we might think as we try to block out the shame, *you gotta break a few eggs*.

In *The Art of Happiness at Work*, His Holiness the 14th Dalai Lama talks about the importance of maintaining our integrity at work:

> When we cultivate compassion, the primary beneficiary is really ourselves. After all, humans are social animals; we are built to work cooperatively with others for our survival. No matter how powerful a single person may be, without other human

companions, that individual person cannot survive. So, at work, if you have a warm heart, human affection, your mind will be calmer and more peaceful, which will give you a certain strength and also allow your mental faculties to function better, your judgement and decision-making abilities and so on.

What His Holiness fails to mention here, in the nicest possible way, is that we need to cultivate our self-worth, self-compassion and self-care so we can be confident enough to have compassion at work. If we're wandering around exhausted and edgy, worrying about who might be out to get us, it's going to be virtually impossible to have a warm heart and human affection.

Taking responsibility for your self-worth isn't about ignoring feedback or being precious about criticism. This is where *work* and *worth* must be separated. By all means, allow more qualified, intelligent people to judge your work, but not your worth. That job belongs to you alone. A bad patch at work doesn't mean your life is going badly, or that you are a bad person; it means work is going badly. Work is not your life.

Perspective is the first step to finding work-life balance. We need to put work in its place. Though its importance will vary in different stages of our lives, it's never appropriate for work to be our whole life. Work is something we do; it's not who we are. Like everything else, jobs are impermanent. No matter how good we are at them, one day they will be gone from our lives. As we've seen, many of the jobs we do now won't even exist one day. If we've built our lives around our work and nothing else, nothing else is what we'll be left with when it ends.

Everybody wants a happy life and a peaceful mind, but we have to produce peace of mind through our own practice.

THE DALAI LAMA

When I was abusing the lollipop lady, in my wound-up state I was sort of determined to prove how hellish my Tuesdays were. When I really got down to my true feelings, Hellish Tuesdays were clear evidence that my life was overwhelming. They proved to me, and hopefully to the people to whom I complained about them, that I was struggling to cope. I guess my hope was that someone would step in and save me if those Hellish Tuesdays got bad enough. But I had to face what I've always known: I needed to be my own saviour. I'm very bad at asking for help, but the fact is that no-one can help me when it comes to my own quirky mind and the creative ways it tries to problem-solve. I needed to save myself from what Buddha called my 'delusions'.

When we look at the world through a Buddhist lens, we start to see that a lot of what we assume is fact is really just our interpretation of the world and our place in it. That's why we disagree with others so much!

I have a friend who found out in his thirties that he was colourblind. As far as he knew, that shade of grey he identified as red was the same thing his friends saw as red. When he was a baby, his mother would point to things and say, 'Red,' like all mothers do, which is how he learnt to call that particular shade of grey 'red'. He and I can both identify red things, but what we are seeing is very different. In fact, all of us see colours at least slightly differently. This is why we sometimes argue over whether something is more red or orange, more blue or purple. It's both, and neither. It's actually completely empty of anything but our interpretation of what it is. Both my friend and I have been living with the delusion that we know what the colour red looks like, and that anyone who sees something different is 'wrong'.

On the day of my run-in with the lollipop lady, there were a number of delusions clouding my perception.

- It was deluded to think the world was against me.

- It was deluded to think being late was a disaster.

- It was deluded to think yelling at someone in the street (or anywhere else) was reasonable.

- It was deluded to think being grumpy with my kids would be helpful to my state of mind.

- It was deluded to think my family should have read my mind and known I needed help.

- It was deluded to think that happiness was something I could catch if I just chased it hard enough.

> The difference between happy people
> and unhappy people is interpretation.

It was deluded to think that arriving exactly on schedule for Louie's class was worth losing my mind and stressing my kids over. If it was impossible to get there on time, then I needed to get a different time – it was that simple. Though it's common to freak out over being late, when you really think about it, it's usually not a big deal. Traffic jams are often caused by terrible car accidents – *that's* a big deal. Thinking about the awful changes someone's life is undergoing in that moment is enough to make me chill out about running late. The challenge is remembering to think about others in those moments.

It was deluded to think that yelling at the lollipop lady was okay under any circumstances. I desperately wanted one of the other school mums to make me feel like my parking illegally and fighting in the street was reasonable, balanced behaviour, but of course it wasn't. It was the behaviour of someone who was drowning, and I don't believe that drowning should be accepted as an inevitable part of life.

Just like we fetishise unbelievable busyness, we've fallen into a trap of glamorising the symptoms of drowning, such as screaming at our kids, disconnecting from our partners and relying on alcohol for relief. Don't get me wrong, I find a good mum/wine meme hilarious, but I think those signs of deep imbalance should be taken seriously. They should encourage us to step back and rethink things because the way we're living isn't working. Are we doing more than we

can cope with? Do we just keep adding tasks and responsibilities and never subtracting ones that are no longer
necessary? Are we sticking steadfastly to rules we made up
for ourselves that don't make sense anymore? Do we have
support we forget to utilise? I am very guilty of immediately
turning down offers of help without properly considering
them. Do you do the same? Or do you swing the other way,
being quick to offer help that you really don't have the time
or energy to give?

It was deluded to think that the world was against me
when I have such a privileged life. When I went to Cambodia, I discovered that it receives the most foreign aid per
citizen of any country in the world, yet women still wander
the streets with their naked babies, begging for food. Many
of those young women have been victims of the country's
roaring child sex trade. They weave dangerously in and out
of Phnom Penh's toxic traffic, which heaves with expensive
foreign cars. Frankly, it's shameful that I should ever think
the world is against *me*.

MINDFULNESS

Freedom from delusions has to start with mindfulness.
We'll discuss mindfulness a lot in our attempt to unravel

our unbelievable busyness. Mindfulness is simply keeping our mind in the current moment instead of letting it wander backwards or forwards in time. It can help us distinguish between what is reasonable future planning, and what is unreasonable. The unreasonable planning, anxiety and worry – aka disturbing emotions – takes us away from the here and now and makes us a lot busier than we need to be.

We have to concentrate on seeing our lives as they really are, if we hope to change them. We have to be brutally honest about our own behaviour too. I know that I love having someone to blame when things go wrong. If I stub my toe on a chair, my first reaction may be to scream at the last person who sat in it. That's not a flattering thing to tell you, but it's true and I can't change it if I ignore it.

This kind of constant critical analysis of our own feelings and actions is really what makes up the 'practice' of Buddhism. It's the grunt work that goes along with the lovely statues and beads. Our quality of life depends entirely on how we engage with life. If we engage with it in a combative, defensive way, hiding behind delusions, then our quality of life will be lessened. If we engage with life without delusions, accepting responsibility for our life as it is and working to improve ourselves, then our quality of life will be increased.

Here's a fantastic mantra for helping you to be in the present:

> When I'm depressed, I'm living in the past,
> When I'm anxious, I'm living in the future.

That's my favourite saying because it highlights the consequences of spending too much time out of the present. We know that this moment is the only one we have any control over, and to focus on the future or the past is to invite disturbance into the mind, and to waste precious energy on things we can't change.

KEY POINTS

- Disturbing emotions are things like anger, fear, jealousy and pride. They create deluded thinking that encourages us to see and engage with the world in a negative light, creating time- and energy-consuming drama.

- We feel disturbing emotions because we're really craving something deeper and harder to satisfy. Disturbing emotions protect our true feelings because they cause us to act out and behave irrationally or destructively, hence creating new problems that distract us from the real issue.

- Investing all our self-worth in work is another disturbing emotion. It can cause us to behave unethically, and prevents us from acting compassionately at work.

- Work and worth must always be separate. Work should never be our whole life.

- We must be responsible for our own self-worth. Relying on others for validation leaves us vulnerable, exhausted and unhappy.

- The same goes for our other disturbing emotions and delusions: only we can free ourselves from them. This is done through mindfulness and seeing our behaviour, thoughts and feelings as they really are.

- The difference between happy people and unhappy people is interpretation. We can choose to react positively or negatively to any given situation.

SELF-REFLECTION

- Take some time to think about how acting out emotionally can make a bad situation worse. Can you think of a recent example from your own life in which you reacted angrily, jealously or fearfully? Looking back, do you think there was a better way to handle the scenario? Make a note of your thoughts.

- What disturbing emotions do you feel the most? When do you tend to feel them? Spend some time thinking about any disturbing emotions you feel around work. This is harder than it sounds and may take days or weeks. Try to notice and name your feelings about work as they arise. Notice which feelings surface most often, and how you tend to behave when they do.

- Take some quiet time to think about your delusions. Make a list of things you treat as fact, even though they are open to interpretation. If you tend to look at things in a negative way, think of a few recent situations in which you felt unbelievably busy and stressed, and try to imagine choosing a more positive and helpful way of looking at them.

7

I'M THE

Unbelievably Busy

SINGLE MOTHER OF
EIGHT-YEAR-OLD TWINS

I feel slightly guilty calling myself a 'single mother' because my ex-husband is so supportive and present in our kids' lives. I have many married friends whose husbands are far less available to them and their children than Adrian is to our family. He is an artist, which means he earns very little money, but can pick the kids up from school when they're sick. You win some; you lose some.

Before anyone is tempted to engage their outrage and accuse me of sexism or maternal martyrdom, let me assure you I'm not suggesting that no-one else in the world can be as busy as a mother. But it's undeniable that becoming one definitely added to my unbelievable busyness. Before motherhood, I generally enjoyed my level of busyness; since my kids, however, it's become a very distressing and depressing burden.

I suspect that much of the intense busyness I've experienced since my twins were born has come from selfishness on my part, because I haven't been prepared to give up much of my pre-motherhood life. However, I also believe that I need to maintain my own identity and life outside of the home, for their sake as much as for mine.

What's the point of generation after generation of women sacrificing their careers and passions for their children, if their daughters only grow up and do the same? I've never understood that. I genuinely believe it's important for me to show my children, particularly my daughter, that a woman can set lofty goals and achieve them without missing out on building a loving family.

I have to admit, though, there have been days when I wondered if it really was possible for women to have it all. I wondered if the only way to raise children and have a career was through two adults each assuming responsibility for one of those things. Yes, what I'm referring to is an old-fashioned partnership in which one parent takes on the responsibility of making money, and the other one takes care of everything to do with the family. Given that men still earn 30 per cent more than women for doing the same jobs, and they don't physically need to take a break from their careers for pregnancy, guess who usually ends up keeping the home fires burning? And guess who ends up with no career or superannuation when they divorce? And guess why statistics show that over half a million Australian women will face homelessness over the next two decades?

It's pretty grim, isn't it? Even if I wanted to, I don't have the option of taking a few years off to focus on my kids, and I don't know many women who do.

So, the question is: where is the line between valuing my life outside of motherhood, and engaging adequately with the lives of my children?

Like many working mothers, I felt as though I was trying to live two lives at once, and neither was functioning. I was tired, grouchy, uninspired and resentful both at home and at work, and feeling like I was failing to some degree at everything.

And as my kids have got older, not only do they demand more but also others demand more on their behalf. Their

teachers constantly ask to meet with me about their progress, even though my kids have a father with more than
enough time on his hands for a chat. I've checked with other
mums at the same school, and in families in which the dad
works full-time, he is never asked to attend these meetings.
So why aren't I treated like dads who work similar hours to
mine? I want to be treated like a dad, damn it! I want to be
worshipped when I show up to a Monday assembly to see
my kid get a prize. I want to be congratulated when I run
my kids' birthday party. I want to be lusted after when I
volunteer to help at the end-of-term disco. But I'm a mum.
It's all just expected of me.

Recently, as I was pulling into a parking space at my local
shops, I saw a man with a small baby strapped to his chest
and a toddler running around his legs. He was loading gro-
ceries into the boot of his car, and, God help me, my heart
melted. I seriously considered jumping out to both help and
congratulate him, but then I realised that I wouldn't have
looked twice at a woman in the same predicament.

I was shocked by my reaction, so I sat in the car for
a minute to try to figure it out. I thought that man was
magnificent because I subconsciously believe that men, in
general, are completely hopeless, panicking babies. What

that man was doing seemed like such an immense achievement because, as a man, it took so much more effort and courage than it would take a woman. I'm not joking here – I swear that was my instinctive response to watching a man attempt a useful activity, particularly involving children. So yes, I was complaining about sexism while harbouring some pretty dumb sexist attitudes of my own. And they add to my unbelievable busyness because they make me carry the load of the men in my life.

My ex is very hands-on with the kids, but he is what I would describe in my sexist way as hopeless, haphazard and lazy. As an example, I remember I'd been in Cambodia for about three days when our babies were twelve months old. My husband sent me a photo in which my son was wearing the same T-shirt I'd put on him before I left. Yes, he'd slept in it, eaten in it, rolled on the floor with the dog in it, etc., for three days. But you know what? He was alive and well when I got home, so I had to acknowledge that there was no harm done, even though his father and I had very different ideas of what looking after children entailed.

Since the birth of our kids, I'd become increasingly resentful of his failure to chip in with the jobs I'd invented, and he was resentful of the superfluous jobs I kept inventing. He felt

I was making more work for myself than I needed to, and then expecting him to share the load.

I'm not advocating not bathing babies for days on end, but I will say that what happened while I was in Cambodia made me reconsider the little jobs I was burdening myself with every day (particularly as I saw so many babies on my trip who were living their little lives without any clothes on at all). Did I have to change our twins so often, and dress them in perfectly clean and matching little jammies every night? Did I have to change the whole outfit if a nappy leaked into the pants, just so they'd never wear mismatched clothes? Did I have to do so much washing every day?

Where the kids are concerned, part of my unbelievable busyness stemmed from my high standards, and the begrudging joy I took from the idea that 'no-one but me does things properly'.

I never asked for help from my kids' father because he wouldn't do things the way I like them done. Not only that, he couldn't even offer to help because I wouldn't tell him more than he absolutely needed to know about our family's daily routine. I kept the whole spreadsheet in my head, including for Hellish Tuesdays. When I felt completely overwhelmed by it all, I'd lash out and accuse him of not shouldering his share of the load, but later, when I'd had a chance to look at the situation intellectually, I had to admit that he had no way of knowing how hideous my Tuesdays were because I'd never told him. I did think about him a lot on Tuesdays, though, usually when I was stuck in traffic with squabbling kids behind me, my white knuckles wrapped around the steering wheel. Oh yeah, he definitely popped into my mind. I'd imagine him wandering around his quiet little house, sipping tea and talking to the cat. BASTARD!

I'll admit, I made myself busier than necessary just by assuming responsibility for stuff that I actually could've got help with. I was doing more than I needed to, and I also felt more alone than I needed to.

I realised that, to paraphrase myself from earlier, there's no point in me missing my children grow up, just so that they can grow up and do the same to their own children. If there's no greater purpose to my unbelievable busyness, if it's just causing an endless cycle of unhappiness for me and my kids and my possible grandkids, then it has to stop. And if it's making me feel crying-in-the-shower tired by homework time then it *definitely* has to stop, because my kids are only in Grade 2. Homework time ain't going away any time soon.

KEY POINTS

- Unbelievable busyness can come from trying to juggle life as a parent and life outside the family. It takes a lot of effort to try to maintain an independent identity while also being a supportive, present and engaged parent.

- Society assumes that women will do the majority of parenting and household duties, whereas men aren't expected to do anywhere near the same amount. This is regardless of how many hours of paid work either parent does.

- In turn, women often internalise these expectations and assume responsibility for tasks that could be shared with their partner. This leads to us feeling unbelievably busy.

- Often this unwillingness to delegate is linked to our self-worth and pride: 'No-one but me does things properly.'

- Resentment can develop when women feel that they're doing all the household work, and men feel that women are doing unnecessary household duties and then expecting men to share them.

SELF-REFLECTION

- Think about how much of your family-related unbelievable busyness comes from your refusal to ask for help, or unwillingness to accept the way other people do things. How much time and energy could you save yourself if you relaxed your standards in this area?

- Ask yourself if you feel resentful towards someone for not helping you. Have you ever actually requested their help, or even let them know you're struggling? Give it a try now. Give them a chance to not let you down.

CASE STUDY:

Chloe

'I'm an unbelievably busy stay-at-home mum, but everyone thinks I'm a "rich bitch" who does nothing all day.'

Chloe is a SAHM. I didn't know what that was either when I first read it on an American woman's blog, but I can now tell you it stands for Stay At Home Mom (or Mum).

Unlike in the '80s, SAHMs are now very much in fashion, only this time the ideal is a woman who has chosen not to work yet is still able to afford an enviable lifestyle. She must keep us constantly updated via social media to show that she's not home on the couch watching infomercials all day long. She's a centred, balanced free spirit, who's in touch with all the things that life's really about, and she has a million social media followers to prove it!

At this stage in my life, I'd kill to be a SAHM, as long as I could live the mummy-blogger, Instagram-influencer lifestyle. As far as I can make out, being a SAHM is all about activewear, chai lattes and high ponytails. If I was a SAHM, I'd meditate for an hour every day, then exercise for another hour before taking a few snaps of my home-grown veggies and blogging about using them to cure all my children's ailments. In the afternoon I'd have some reiki or cupping, meet some other cool SAHMs for another chai and some sit-ups, and then fetch my kids from school for some paleo snacks at home and fun with educational toys I've made myself out of hemp and coconut oil. I'd just be really happy and chilled out, all the damn time.

Does anyone really get to live like that? Well, I used to think my friend Chloe did, and I was so jealous!

CHLOE

Chloe became a hairdresser at fifteen, and had her own salon by the time she was twenty-two. But the bulk of her family's fortune was made by her husband, who has one of those jobs that has been explained to me many times and yet I still don't really know what it is. I know he helps companies do something and he travels a lot. I know they have a big house and nice cars and Chloe doesn't have to work anymore.

Why am I telling you this annoying story, I hear you ask? I'm telling you because Chloe is unbelievably busy. I shit you not.

Chloe is constantly racing to drop a kid off and/or pick a kid up, and she always has someone else's kids with her. Chloe is the organiser of every event at the school, the football club, the dancing school and her mum's assisted living village. Chloe often has to cancel her own plans because her husband has stayed away longer than expected, or her neighbour is having a crisis and needs her help, or her son's pet axolotl is looking peaky.

Every family event is held at Chloe's house and she's always on catering duties, alone. Her sisters and sisters-in-law work, so Chloe insists that she has more time to deal with this stuff; they, of course, are quite happy to let her. Every religious holiday, birthday, anniversary and post-funeral afternoon tea is project-managed and presented by Chloe. It works out at about two major events a month, now that her older children are in the latter stages of high school. They're too young to go out and drink but too old for play dates, so they have 'gatherings' (smaller and less risky than a party, apparently) during which they pretend to be adults by Chloe's pool while she serves them mocktails and hors d'oeuvres. Chloe's husband thinks she's mad for indulging the gatherings, but she says she'd rather they stay at home where she can keep an eye on them. (My mum used to say the same thing, but we were lucky to get a takeaway pizza out of her!)

Chloe's always up bright and early on weekends to take the younger ones to soccer and footy, which are never played at the same ground but frequently scheduled close together, so she has to duck and weave through the thousands of other harried parents on the roads on Saturday and Sunday mornings to drop them off and pick them up on time. The younger boys are still very much in play-date territory and insist on having mates over most Saturday afternoons. By the time they get back from sport, the teenage tigress and the monosyllabic big brother will have awoken and they'll all be grumpily foraging for food in the kitchen.

'There's nothing to eat here!' they'll cry, before breaking into a wrestling match and spreading mud and teenage stink all over Chloe's clean kitchen. She'll then fix their hunger for them, either whipping up something or running to the shops. Heaven forbid her younger sons' friends go home with stories of deprivation!

Every mum who comes to pick up her son will stay for a coffee and a chat, and before she knows it Chloe will be running slightly behind on her night-time schedule: kids in baths, clothes in washing machine, another meal to cook and clean up after, the tigress delivered to someone else's gathering, clothes on the line, screen time to argue over, husband to pay attention to, axolotl tank to clean, and the tigress to bring home.

My work schedule gets me out of doing pretty much all of that, although my children's lack of both sporting prowess and interest are just lucky breaks. No Saturday morning sports for us so far, thank goodness, and I swear to God if one of them wants to take up competitive swimming, I'm out. Do you know what time those kids get to the pool every morning? Mind you, if I were to be so unlucky as to have the next Ian Thorpe on my hands, I could probably just ask Chloe to deal with it. She would comply because the poor darling woman has lost the capacity to say 'no'.

It turns out that people are really resistant to hearing you're tired and unbelievably busy when you don't have a job. Because she feels like she doesn't have a valid reason to say no, Chloe says yes, all the time, to everything.

Chloe's husband, Luke, gets irritated by having to fend off constant invitations. 'Another dinner with parents from school?' he moans. 'Another trivia night?'

'I hate going to these things alone,' Chloe mumbled once.

'Well, some of us have jobs to go to in the morning, babe,' Luke replied firmly.

It was a stinging response, but one she was used to. She heard it often from people who felt overwhelmed in their own lives and took the opportunity to exercise their jealousy over the life they thought she led. Of course, she wasn't obnoxious enough to see it that way – she internalised it every time, and let it chip away at her self-worth.

On top of being frequently belittled by her husband and friends, Chloe felt guilty about her life and constantly tried to prove it hadn't made her a spoilt, rich bitch.

'Rich bitch' was a phrase Chloe's mum used regularly when she'd return home from her job cleaning houses. Chloe's mum talked a lot about the frivolous lifestyles of the families she worked for, about the 'brats' who never made their own beds, the 'slimeball' husbands who were probably sleeping with their secretaries, and the 'rich bitch' mums who were too lazy to clean their own houses.

When she was young, Chloe would roll her eyes at her mum's negative assumptions about her clients. 'Have they ever been home when you were there?' she'd ask, chuckling. 'How do you know he's a slimeball?'

'They're all like that up there,' her mum would snort, nodding towards the nice part of town (which, incidentally, is where both Chloe and her mum live today).

Her mum certainly didn't think Luke was a slimeball when he first started coming around. Handsome, well educated and well travelled, Luke was already impressing his corporate overlords when he wandered into Chloe's salon one afternoon, hoping for a trim. A couple of months later, he was brought home to meet her parents, and Chloe's mum couldn't have been happier to have him in the family.

He had the unmistakable air of someone who'd grown up without money troubles invading family life. He was laid-back and charming, he could hold a conversation with anyone about anything, and he insisted that Chloe's noisy, impolite, sometimes farty family was fun, which was not the word she used to describe them.

Luke lived in a tiny flat that was always freezing in winter and hideously hot in summer, but he never complained. He seemed to find it amusing. Everything was an adventure for

Luke, even down to the smallest inconvenience, like having to carry a basket of heavy, wet clothes down to the laundrette when his washing machine broke down mid-cycle. He laughed all the way, probably because he knew he could afford to buy a new one as soon as the shops opened on Monday. Luke had the confidence of someone for whom everything had always worked out pretty well, and it was such a startling counterpoint to her mother's bitter pessimism that Chloe soon found herself wanting to spend every moment with him. So he would remain relaxed and carefree, she waited on him hand and foot, and tried to fix every little problem that popped up in his life.

Chloe found a nicer flat for them to live in together and organised the movers. She packed and unpacked everything herself, and cooked a bang-up meal for the two of them on their first night as live-in lovers. Luke was in heaven, of course, and, assuming it would all work out well, he asked her to marry him. After their wedding, they honeymooned in Europe and discovered they were having a baby, all within three years of that first fateful haircut.

Luke and Chloe decided that she would sell the salon and become a full-time mum for a while. 'I'll probably go back when the baby goes to school,' she said at the time, but more babies followed and before she knew it, she'd been a decade out of the workforce, so unbelievably busy taking care of people that she didn't know how she'd ever find the time or the energy to go back to work.

By that stage, both Chloe's and Luke's parents were elderly and in need of varying levels of help. As the only adult without work commitments, Chloe was the one they called upon if they needed to be driven somewhere or to have something brought over for them.

She and Luke found a lovely place near them for her parents. It was very high-end assisted living and cost them a fortune but, when the mood took her, Chloe's mum wasn't above accusing her of dumping her there to die. Once, when Chloe had been too busy to take her mum on an outing to the local plaza, the old lady snarled, 'I don't know how you rich bitches fill your days. I was raising four kids and working six days a week at your age.'

It cuts pretty deep to hear your mother say you've become the kind of person she despises. Luke laughed it off when Chloe told him, as is his habit. 'Just ignore her, babe,' he said, trying to soothe her. 'Take her to the shops next week and she'll forget about it.'

Luke generally didn't worry about what other people thought of him. He wasn't conceited – he simply thought he was a good person, doing his best, and he was happy with that. Chloe, on the other hand, was increasingly obsessed with how other people saw her. Did they think she was a rich bitch because she didn't have a job? Did they think she was lazy and spoilt? Caught between two very different world-views – her husband's and her mother's – Chloe somehow trusted her mother's more, probably because it had been ingrained in her since childhood. As much as she wanted to embrace Luke's gentle, unassuming confidence, she found herself increasingly worried about how other people saw her.

As a result, Chloe ramped up her generosity and took every job going when it came to kids activities. She specialised in the ones most of us run a mile from. She was treasurer of everything – that's the job no-one wants. It's a role with real responsibility, and you can't slack off and miss a meeting or two (not that Chloe would've dreamt of it). She was always the first to arrive and the last to leave, usually with several pieces of Tupperware under her arms, having baked all afternoon.

Chloe became known far and wide as a no-phobe, which meant that she was completely taken advantage of to make up for mums like me who never get involved in anything. Chloe was the first port of call when the footy team needed to raise some money, when the school wanted parents to supervise a disco, or when the in-laws couldn't turn on their iPad. No-one even bothered asking anyone else, because they knew Chloe would do it and do it well.

Luke noticed his children's behaviour moving in a direction he didn't like. One night he walked through the front door just in time to see a roll of cling wrap flying across the living room towards Chloe. It bounced off the wall beside her head, and the house fell silent as everyone turned to look towards the kitchen, where the tigress stood, red-faced and furious. Luke's head tipped to the side, like he was a confused Labrador, and his daughter let out a bellow and slammed the nearest cupboard door. 'I can't take it here anymore. I want to go to boarding school!'

Every set of eyes then swung around to Luke, who knew that, for the first time since she was born, *he* was going to have to seriously discipline his daughter. This responsibility had always fallen to Chloe, primarily because he was never around to see the tigress misbehaving. When they were all young, the kids were ready for bed by the time he got home, and the day's fights had been fought and won. As the children got older, and Luke earned the right to travel less and leave work earlier, he saw more of the day-to-day politics of the household, and he wasn't always proud of what he saw.

He saw children who expected to be waited on by their mother, and he reflected guiltily on how readily he'd let her do the same for him. He saw Chloe rushing to fulfil the family's every wish before going out to attend some meeting or taking one of the boys to footy training in the rain. Luke saw how the family had outgrown agreements they'd made when expecting their first child.

Luke asked the tigress what the hell was going on, and she didn't hesitate to bring him up to speed on her mother's shortcomings. They included Chloe's refusal to allow a boyfriend sleepover, Chloe's attempt to instigate a clothing budget, Chloe's failure to buy the fat-free ice-cream bars she'd been instructed to, Chloe's supposed lack of time to conduct a driving lesson, and Chloe's insistence on finding out more information about a student exchange program to America before paying the deposit.

What. A. Bitch.

Then the tigress dropped an insult he found shamefully familiar. 'How can you be so tired and busy all the time, Mum? I mean, it's not like you have to go to work or school every day like the rest of us.'

Luke's mood turned pretty dark in that moment. He quickly defended Chloe against all of their daughter's accusations before sending the tigress upstairs, with the rather abstract instruction to think about how much her mother does for her.

It was a watershed moment for the family. Having his dismissive attitude towards his wife's life reflected back at him by their daughter wasn't Luke's proudest moment. Knowing the younger boys were soaking it all up like little sponges was heavy, too. Both Chloe and Luke sensed it was a character-shaping moment in their children's lives, and they weren't quite sure how to spin it in a positive direction.

Was it going to be okay to throw things at Mum from now on? Would it be accepted that Mum's not having a job meant her life was less meaningful and that she existed just to serve others?

The littlest boy, who was actually a bit scared by the volatility in the house, broke the stunned silence left behind as the tigress stomped upstairs and slammed her bedroom door.

'Let her go to America, Mum,' he said, throwing his arms around Chloe's waist, with tears in his eyes. 'Let them keep her.'

Teenage girls are the devil's back-up dancers, we all know that, and while many parents would no doubt love to send them to another country between the ages of about thirteen and twenty, it's our difficult duty to try to steer them through it, while simultaneously keeping the rest of the family intact. A separate and much deeper problem for Chloe's family was the idea that she had nothing going on in her life when she was patently unbelievably busy. The pervasive falsehood was making the children entitled and disrespectful, and was decimating Chloe's self-image.

In a moment of clarity, as Chloe looked down at that loving little boy wrapped around her, she realised he was well and truly old enough to set the table for dinner.

She'd been desperately trying to get dinner on the table when the chaos had broken out. Every night she cooked it, served it, took complaints about it and then cleaned up after it. On this night, though, she decided she was going to sit quietly on the back steps for a few minutes, and she asked Luke to coordinate dinner.

Well, he was hardly going to say no, was he?

He and the boys clumsily but good-naturedly set the table and dished up dinner. The little one tapped Chloe gently on the shoulder and invited her in to eat, and when she was done, she announced she was going upstairs for a bath while they rinsed the plates and stacked the dishwasher.

For the first time in her life, Chloe didn't make sure her daughter had some dinner. Instead, she lay in the hot bath, thinking about the sixteen years of dinners she'd slaved over for that girl, and she filled with pride. Chloe knew she was a great mum, and she knew that her kids were very lucky to have her.

Chloe remembered the dramas of her own teenage years, and chuckled over things she'd thought were important and real. She tried to look at herself through teenage eyes, and she had an epiphany. She didn't care what her daughter thought of her. Not in that moment, on that night, because her daughter was not a reasonable judge.

Chloe realised she had nothing to feel ashamed of where her daughter was concerned. As much as she loved her, she knew her daughter was a seething mass of hormones, privilege and acne. Why would any reasonable person allow their self-worth to be dampened by a teenage girl? In fact, why would any reasonable person allow their self-worth to be dampened by *anyone*?

Chloe suddenly understood Luke's outlook. Deep down, she knew she was a good person doing her best, and she didn't deserve a roll of cling wrap flying towards her head. Anyone who tried to make her feel otherwise was being an arsehole of the highest order.

Chloe faced the reality that the amount of effort she put in for others was not proportionate to their respect or gratitude for her. Chloe's kids, parents and husband didn't love and respect her more on days she did more for them. If anything, it tended to work the opposite way: the more she gave, the more they expected, and the more likely they were to be disappointed if she failed to live up to the high standard she'd set.

No-one ever said, 'It's okay you forgot the low-fat ice-cream bars today, and by the way, I just want to thank you for the beautiful smoothie you made me yesterday.'

Yesterday's generosity was forgotten, the slate wiped clean, and every new day was another endurance test. She didn't even like herself more when she did more. So what was the point?

For the first time in ages, Chloe asked herself, 'What do I want to be doing with my life? What kind of person do I want to be?'

After the bath, Chloe lay down on her bed in a towel. Her whole body was pulsing from the hot water, and she breathed deeply and relaxed. She thought about those blogs she'd read about the importance of 'me' time and self-care. She thought about all the guided meditations and wellness ideas she'd emailed to herself, meaning to read them later but never getting around to it, and about all the scented candles she'd been gifted for volunteering her time, encouraging her to indulge in some quiet, perfumed reflection.

She listened to her youngest sons clanging crockery around downstairs and chattering away happily to their dad. She resolved to find ways to support her kids without giving them the impression she was their personal slave. She wrote out a quote she'd read on a blog once that said, 'It's a parent's job to make themselves obsolete in their children's lives.' Later, she stuck it on the fridge for the benefit of everyone in the family.

'What sort of adults have we been building?' she asked Luke when he tapped the paper on the fridge and looked at her quizzically. 'What sort of adults do we want to build?'

Chloe acknowledged the ways in which her own parents had got it right. She thought about how their parenting had made her independent, and vowed to give her own kids the same gift. While she was at it, she'd gift her children with public transport cards.

Chloe's new goal of parental obsolescence became a creative endeavour for the whole family. She taught the children to cook, which they enjoyed, and she taught them to clean, which they hated but they had so many perks that she was never short of electronics to confiscate or gatherings to cancel if responsibilities weren't met.

The quote on the fridge was soon joined by a roster, and though she was still the primary housekeeper, household duties were definitely being shared around more. The kids developed signature dishes and proudly invited their friends over to watch them cook. They were even savvy enough to work out their least loathed cleaning duties and swap among themselves accordingly.

At Chloe's insistence, weekly allowances were set, bank accounts were opened and savings goals were instituted. Chloe and Luke rewarded their kids' savings efforts by chipping in towards various dreams, from first cars to gaming consoles to skateboards.

The gatherings continued but Chloe added a condition: they had to be catered for and cleaned up by the kids and their friends. If the kids failed to do this, the gatherings would stop and the kids wouldn't be allowed to attend other gatherings either. Of course, the tigress thought the idea of combining her friends and her mother in any capacity was a recipe for social suicide, but she was forced to accept the deal by her friends, who leapt at the chance to learn how to whip up gourmet party food in Chloe's beautiful kitchen. It all felt so grown up to don an apron and prepare a party, and they were proud of their Instagrammable efforts.

(Side question: why do we always think everyone else's mums are perfectly delightful human beings, but our own mums are embarrassing weirdos who should be gagged and hidden in the linen cupboard when our friends are around?)

Every night after dinner, while the rostered dishwasher-stacker was going about their duties, Chloe slid back into that bath, by the light of one of those smelly candles. She was usually in there for about half an hour, and though the tranquillity was often disturbed by some kind of blood-curdling battle raging downstairs, Luke had accepted responsibility for matters of war during her bath time.

The other big change was that she didn't have to go out to meetings on weeknights anymore because she'd resigned from every one of the committees and working groups she'd been part of. It was actually Luke who finally convinced her that she'd done her bit, and that she had nothing to be ashamed of in taking more time for herself. 'Let someone else chip in,' he said, and she'd had to admit he was right. The various funding shortfalls and disco duties weren't her personal responsibility. They were the responsibility of the entire community, and it was time for others to step in.

Chloe thought the hardest part would be saying no to good people, and she dreaded it, but she'd underestimated the universality of the unbelievable busyness she was trying to deal with. Once she was honest about the ridiculous amount of responsibilities she'd taken on, everyone she spoke to understood and empathised completely. They were all in the same boat, of course. They were all trying to keep up with their ever-changing impermanent lives, trying to make the best of their resources and work positively towards their futures. They got it!

Who knows what the future will bring for this family? Maybe Chloe will go back to work at some point, and maybe she won't. She has definitely managed to change her present, though, and to develop a sense of self-respect without needing to single-handedly run her family, the school, the junior football league and the teenage social club for the entire community.

8

I'M AN
Unbelievable Ex-wife

Let's face it: romantic relationships are hard work. If they're going well, it takes a lot of time and energy to maintain them. And if they're *not* going well, you can find yourself unbelievably busy either trying to ignore it, or trying to fix it.

I remember accusing my ex of making my already difficult life harder with his 'carry on'. Just listening to him talk sometimes felt like an extra job that was keeping me from something else. There was a time, of course, when I longed to listen to him talk! That's good old Impermanence in action yet again.

Sadly, yes, I am an ex-wife now, after being a wife for nineteen years. I can still get emotional about it if I try hard enough – I can miss the great days of our marriage, in which I felt completely loved and supported by someone who really knew me and liked me anyway. Time has healed me a lot, though. I used to find myself daydreaming about nice memories from my marriage until I thought my heart would just give up and ooze out of the bottom of my trousers and into the nearest drain, but that doesn't really happen much anymore. I still think it's a shame the marriage ended, but I don't long for it, nor do I keep begging him to love me again.

My unbelievable busyness built steadily over the course of our marriage, but of course it exploded when we had kids. Before that, every moment I wasn't working was devoted to Adrian, but naturally that changed when our two babies arrived. From that day on it was babies first, second and third, with work maybe fourth, and then sleep taking every other position on the priority list.

If we ever did manage some leisure time, all we really wanted to do was be alone with ourselves, not with each other. Pretty rapidly he'd excuse himself to find a drink and I'd curl up in bed with my phone to quietly scroll my life away. We were both looking for escape and, frankly, I just didn't have anything left to give.

The rigours of keeping a relationship alive are part of the overall busyness that threatens to consume you. To keep growing with another person takes time, attention and energy – all of which are in short supply in our busy lives. We might summon those forces, but at different times to our partners, making it seem like we're never able to connect anymore. We may feel like we're not prioritised in their lives. When we dig down, we may discover we've been taking them for granted. We may even realise we've been using unbelievable busyness as an excuse to avoid ending a relationship we no longer want.

When we say that other people or situations 'make' us happy or sad, angry or relaxed, we are misunderstanding our minds and bestowing far too much power onto others. In the same way that we can place all our self-worth in work, we can invest all our happiness and self-respect in our romantic relationships. And, just like at work, this can add to our unbelievable busyness as we waste time and energy chasing happiness and fulfilment outside of ourselves.

When we feel happy in the presence of our partners, it's often because being with them tells us something we like about ourselves. Perhaps we think we must be interesting, good-looking, sexy, smart or kind for this person to choose to spend time with us. This idea creates happiness in us. The other person hasn't cast a spell to 'make' us happy. That's impossible, as anyone who's tried to comfort a child who's lost a cherished toy will tell you. If there was a way to 'make' people happy, parents would give everything they own to know what it was. It doesn't exist. Happiness cannot exist in a person who refuses to be happy. Satisfaction cannot exist in a person who refuses to be satisfied. Unbelievable busyness cannot end for a person who refuses to let it go.

In terms of romantic happiness, I present this quote from Ed O'Neill's *Modern Family* character, Jay Pritchett, the prickly patriarch who occasionally drops powerful truth-bombs about the human condition:

> Why do we choose partners so different from ourselves? It's not fate or chance or cliches like, 'The heart wants what the heart wants.' We choose our partners because they represent the unfinished business from our childhood. And we choose them because they manifest the qualities we wish we had. In doing so, in choosing such a challenging partner and working to give them what they need, we chart a course for our own growth.

Happiness isn't gifted to us by our partners; it comes from a feeling of achievement and wish-fulfilment within ourselves. If we rely on our relationship for our happiness, it will ebb and flow because people change, and those changes don't always gel with our perception of ourselves and who we want to be. If our self-worth is reflected in the desirability of our partner, it can even wane over the course of a night!

We've all been on dates with our partners that have started off well, as we've admired them all dressed up and handsome, but that have turned into a nightmare after too many drinks, haven't we? A night where we started out happily married to a charming gentleman and ended up miserably apologising for an obnoxious, socially inept fool? Please tell me we've all had that.

Ideally, we should be happy regardless of the success of our partner's evening, but typically our own egos are pretty tied up with their performance, so we watch on nervously, hoping they'll be someone we can be proud of for most of the night, and that we'll spot the turning point in time to call an Uber and get them out of there without incident.

Happiness in relationships comes easily at times, and comes only with a great deal of effort at other times. If a tough relationship period happens to coincide with an unbelievably busy work period, as well as any kind of parenting, it feels like something's gotta give. In my case, I had to give up on the relationship. It took me years, don't get me wrong. I tried to make it work for a really long time, but in the end I had to cut it loose. I could have stopped working, I suppose, but that would have made us very broke, and raising kids with no money generally doesn't improve a relationship.

Our desire for happiness is strong, our desire for people we fall in love with is intoxicating, and we tend to try to ignore changes in those relationships for as long as possible because they're so scary.

As we know, Buddha believed that desire is the root of all our suffering. Our longing – *Upadana* – for things, for people and for certain feelings keeps us unhappy. We are unhappy if we never get what we want, and if we do get what we want, we just want more!

I must admit that almost from the minute I decided to give up on my marriage, I felt a huge burden lift from my shoulders. Since then, I've been able to concentrate on my relationship with my kids, instead of trying to work around them to get to their father and work on him, and as a result my home life is much more peaceful and simple.

I've had to simplify because I no longer have a husband to pick up the slack from my harebrained attempts at chasing happiness. I rescued an aggressive dog when I was six months pregnant; I invited homeless people to stay with us; I painted the interior of our house in fluorescent yellow and orange. I did all of those things because I thought they'd make me feel good about myself and be happy, but all of them ended up being Adrian's problems to deal with. The aggressive dog bit delivery men and neighbours, but I was never home to hear about it; he eventually had to ask the homeless people to move on, because I was out of town; the walls had to be repainted (by him) because they made us squint and gave us headaches.

I never conferred with my husband before doing any of these things. Hell, I didn't even consult him about having twins! I told the IVF doctor to go ahead and 'chuck two in', without asking Adrian's opinion. That poor man deserves his own peaceful and simple house. His absence forced me to get real about my self-indulgence in chasing happiness and about how much of a burden it was on him.

Though I sometimes miss the marriage we had a long time ago, I don't miss the draining battle it turned into. So now I'm a friendly ex-wife, which also takes time and effort but mostly self-control. I have to be respectful of his time and his privacy, and not swallow him up in my life again.

He is still the person I want to talk to when I'm scared or embarrassed, but now he just shakes his head and smiles like he did way back in the beginning. I'm no longer his responsibility, and I don't pine for him to deal with my excesses anymore. Now I focus on trying not to indulge them in the first place, and that has had a positive impact on my unbelievable busyness over the time since we parted.

KEY POINTS

- Healthy relationships take a lot of energy and hard work to keep them going. This can contribute to you feeling unbelievably busy.

- Unhealthy relationships are even more draining. You could be expending energy trying to make it work, or trying to avoid ending it.

- Relationships can also make us feel unbelievably busy because we're chasing happiness and fulfilment through the relationship, rather than finding it within ourselves.

- Our partners don't make us happy. We feel happy around them because of how we think they view us: as sexy, smart, generous, kind, etc.

- Relationships can suffer if your partner always has to deal with your attempts to chase happiness.

SELF-REFLECTION

- If you are in a relationship, think about how your partner makes you feel. In happy moments, what qualities do you think your partner sees in you? How do you see your partner in those moments?

- If you're single, reflect on your past relationships. Were you seeking something from your exes that you wanted in yourself?

9

I'M CHASING

Success

When His Holiness the 14th Dalai Lama says that all any of us are trying to be is happy, he's talking about the fundamental desire of every living being, whether it's an athlete training for a gold medal, or a spider chasing a fly. Each of us is trying to create happiness for ourselves. Where we tend to come unstuck is in our interpretation of what happiness is and in our willingness to sacrifice the happiness of others to attain our own. Unlike animals, we humans tend to think strategically, obsessing about the future and wallowing in the past, and to see other people's success as threatening to our own. Worst of all, we've tied the idea of *happiness* to the concept of *success*. Ask yourself this: 'Could I feel happy and unsuccessful at the same time?'

What even is success? Like 'happiness', what we consider to be success changes over time. I remember when for me it was being able to ride my bike without training wheels. I was eight years old, which was a bit old to be rocking the training wheels. By that stage my poor mother had spent the previous three years running for miles around our neighbourhood, holding the back of my bike seat and panting, 'Pedal, pedal!'

I've never found engaging my core easy, and as a young child I had the strength of a sedated jellyfish. I could never bring my knees up to wrap them around a monkey bar and hang upside down. My mother said that was a blessing because it meant no-one ever saw my underpants, but I wasn't so sure. I longed to be one of the upside-down girls. Similarly, I longed to ride my bike to school, but couldn't move my legs up and down on the pedals and balance my body at the same time. Then one day, it just happened. On a friend's bike, actually, during a Sunday barbecue, and I can still see the faces of the spectators cheering me on from the driveway. At least half of them were drunk adults, waving tinnies of beer in the air, a hootin' and a hollerin' like I'd single-handedly won a football grand final. Sometimes, even now, all these years later, I summon that image in my mind when I feel like I deserve a cheer squad on the side-lines of my life.

Of course, accompanying our desire for success is our fear of failure. Among the crowd that day was the very sad face of my friend whose parents had recently decided to separate. I'll never forget that little boy's face, racked with pain among the throng of cheering people, oblivious to him. I didn't know about his parents' separation until I commented on his lack of excitement for me on the drive home. Even then, I didn't understand how all-consuming a family break-up is on young children.

Of course, his face floated into my mind many times as I tried to comfort my children during our family break-up. Talk about feeling unsuccessful.

I think that's partly why so many relationship breakdowns become nasty. There's a strong feeling of failure, of being unsuccessful, and the only way to alleviate it is to blame the other person for the whole sorry mess. It's difficult to think we'll find happiness again if we believe we fail at relationships. It's much easier to tell ourselves we now deserve happiness after the disaster our former partner put us through.

Work relationships can go the same way. Very few of us admit to being let go by our employer because we were unsuccessful at the job. That would be crushing and make future happiness difficult to obtain. We're much more likely to move forward by saying, 'That place is run by idiots!' or 'That guy's always hated me!' or 'They just don't like strong women!'

While those things sometimes play a role, we should always apply the theory known as Occam's razor. William of Occam was a fourteenth-century German theologian who came up with the following principle: if there are two or more explanations for an occurrence, the simplest one is usually right.

It's hilarious that such an obvious statement could be lauded as a brilliant moment in philosophy, but if you remember it during the next couple of days, I promise you'll realise just how infrequently we opt for the simplest explanation. 'I'm exhausted because the world is out to get mums' is a classic example of my forgetting Occam's razor.

'I get into car accidents because no-one else can drive.'

'I struggle with relationships because all men are pigs.'

These are pretty commonly held beliefs, aren't they? And do they remind you of anything? Yup, that's right:

these would all fit nicely in the list of delusions we discussed earlier. The fear that arises from a sense of failure is a disturbing emotion that causes us to act out and create new problems, to distract us from dealing with our deeper feelings.

My worst one? 'I'm not happy because I'm not successful enough.'

I had become completely obsessed and overwhelmed by the idea that I had to be successful to be happy – not only for me, but that my children would never be happy if I wasn't successful. That idea kept me unbelievably busy, but it was like chasing a daydream. It took up all my time and energy and it kept me focused on the future instead of the present, blinding me to the moments of happiness that popped up around me all the time. I was chasing success, and not noticing happiness.

There's a Zen Buddhist concept with the lovely name of Shoshin, which means 'beginner's mind'. The idea is to cultivate Shoshin to stop being captive to outdated beliefs, looking afresh at our lives and dealing with them as they really are now.

Without Shoshin, we can easily continue to live in ways that no longer work for us, and we can keep chasing goals that no longer make sense. In this way, we can find we've achieved many goals without achieving happiness. What a waste of energy! How many goals are you chasing because you put them on a mental list when you were twenty years old? I'm a completely different person to who I was back then, so it seems crazy to slavishly still chase those same goals now, doesn't it?

Even ten years ago, I wanted my children to attend a bilingual school because I thought it would be cool, as no-one in our family speaks anything but English. Luckily, their father and his wisdom saved the day yet again. When our kids were approaching school age, he helped me see that the bilingual school was an hour away from home, and that just getting them to the local school half a block away on time every morning was going to be a battle. Not to mention that we were struggling to teach them English, without adding another language that neither of us spoke. Plus, the bilingual school was expensive and the local school was not. If it weren't for Adrian's influence, I'd be so much more unbelievably busy today, on every front!

I gradually realised that I was judging my success on

very narrow, financially focused criteria. AKA, how much stuff I've got. I believed that where there was lots of stuff, happiness was bound to follow – but I never got around to checking for evidence that equation was true. I was far too busy trying to create more success!

I'd say most people think of me as pretty laid-back and down to earth, but in reality I was tightly wound around a pretty shallow success checklist. Let's see if my list rings a bell for you.

To feel truly successful, I would have to:

- have an impressive job

- have a nice house in a nice neighbourhood

- have a nice car

- have some kind of investment making me money

- send my children to a nice school

- have successful children

- have nice holidays

- dress myself and my children in new clothes, all the time

- be able to give my children every faddish childhood accessory, immediately

- be able to give myself every faddish adult accessory, immediately

- have other people think highly of me, and have a reputation as a hard worker

Wow. There's a lot of ego, insecurity and artifice there, isn't there? Not to mention a lot of time and energy – I'm exhausted just reading it! It's pretty clear that I was relying on the outward appearances of success, and on other people's judgements, to create my own happiness. I wanted people to think I was successful and a good person who deserved it all. The trouble with that approach is that you can never be liked and respected by *everyone*, so it follows that you'll never feel totally successful or happy. As we know, you can't hand your self-worth over to other people.

I can see immediately that the success list is all about chasing happiness, whereas the who-I-want-to-be list – which we wrote in the self-reflection at the start of Part 1 – lends itself more towards noticing happiness.

As obsessed as I was with being successful, my cultural background prohibited me from acknowledging my success, let alone enjoying it. Traditionally, Australians who publicly enjoy their achievements are called wankers, although increasingly I hear young people encourage each other to 'own' their successes (however modest) and to publicise them. The Kardashians/Jenners/Wests have made owning success and the conspicuous consumption that goes with it seem humble, as though it's about honesty and openness rather than greed and ego.

Whichever way you swing on that particular issue, my point is that no matter how hard we try we can't create a personality that will be universally liked. Everyone looks at us through the lens of their own worldview, and that's how they decide whom they like and whom they don't. One man's wanker is another man's inspiring success story.

My baby girl, Dali, struggles with this a lot. She's a very peaceful, gentle soul, the kind of kid who people have always looked at and said, 'Oh, she's been here before,' meaning planet Earth, because she seems so wise and settled. She's only eight, but she's always seemed like a grown up in a child's body. She was reasonable even as a newborn. While her brother squirmed and screamed and demanded to be attached to my body 24/7, Dali slept in a bouncer at her father's feet. She'd wake with a smile, have a big stretch, a bottle and a burp, and then go straight back to sleep. 'She sleeps like someone with a clear conscience and an optimistic heart,' I used to say admiringly, while jiggling her brother into submission.

Now she's at the mercy of the playground, and the cruel and random social experimentation of other kids. She likes school and has plenty of friends (although, truth be told, I think she prefers the company of teachers), but every so often she'll become the subject of a nasty comment or a point-and-giggle campaign and it just kills her. She prides herself on her kindness and generosity, so when someone treats her in a way that feels like punishment, it confuses and upsets her. It's so hard watching your children learn about the dumbest bits of human nature, isn't it?

I try to help by saying all the things mums are meant to say – 'Who cares what they think? Just go and play with someone else. They're idiots. They're jealous. Just ignore them.' – but she gets frustrated by my carry-on.

'You don't understand how school works, Mum,' her brother once told me, with a roll of his eyes and a suck of his Chupa Chup.

All I can do is keep advising my girl to be kind to herself, be the best person she can be and not let other people's bullshit get her down. Hopefully it'll sink in at some point over the next thirty years or so, like it did for me. I'm now much better at separating who I really am from who people think I am – I have to be, because strangers sometimes contact me online to tell me what a piece of shit I am. If I let that get to me, I'd have crumbled a long time ago. Having said that, writing the list of my goals for success made me realise I still had some work to do in this area.

There's an old Chinese proverb that says, 'When you finish your house, you die.' I can relate to that because I'm always tinkering with my house, moving furniture and painting walls, etc. I think it's probably the same with personal growth. Just when you think you're finally done and can sit back and admire your handiwork, you turn around and realise you have so much more to do. But trust me – doing the regular checking-in and analysis of our deeper feelings – the daily practice of Buddhism – is WAY better than putting up with a run-down, dilapidated eyesore.

Remember my theory at the start of the book that we're all unbelievably busy because we're chasing happiness? We've already seen how we can exhaust ourselves by placing our happiness in work or our relationships, and now I hope I've convinced you that our busyness also comes from chasing success – more specifically, our Western idea of success as material goods, prosperity and popularity. We were taught these values by our parents – remember my dad and the scratchie debacle? – who focused all their energy on chasing success so as to provide the family with a secure future. It's difficult to confront our unbelievable busyness because society fetishises not only busyness but also material success, so we're encouraged to keep going on all fronts. Things get even MORE complicated because our consumerist society tells us to treat ourselves by buying things or spending big on extravagant holidays, in order to compensate for being so unbelievably busy. So, material success is both the cause of and the solution to our unhappiness! How crazy is THAT?!

All right, take a deep breath. It's going to be okay. Hopefully by now you're starting to understand some of the reasons for your own unbelievable busyness. Now you know you don't have to live like the Hungry Ghost, and you don't have to be trapped by your disturbing emotions and delusions. Even though we live in a society that rewards busyness and material success, you can choose to live in a way that focuses on being present in the moment, noticing happiness and finding genuine fulfilment. In Part 2, we'll now look at what it will take to be unbelievably happy.

SELF-REFLECTION

Take a moment to sit quietly and think about what you're trying to achieve in your life to feel successful. Write your own success checklist. I expect that spiritual growth is part of it, which is why you're holding this book, but go deeper than that. Be brutally honest with yourself. What are the real goals you're pursuing in order to feel successful? Why are you working so hard? Why are you so unbelievably busy?

Take a couple of days with it, if you need to, because it's really important. We need to know what rewards we think we're working towards, so we can figure out if they're worth it or not.

Once you've compiled that success checklist, go back to the self-reflection exercise from the start of the book about what kind of person you want to be. Let's get serious about the ways those two lists complement and contradict each other.

PART 2

WHAT WOULD IT TAKE TO BE

Unbelievably

Happy?

Even in Buddha's day, centuries before our toxic consumerist Western culture, people wrestled with how to incorporate Buddha's teachings into their everyday lives. It was King Suchandra of the Indian kingdom of Shambhala who first raised with Buddha the issue of spirituality in the real world. The king liked Buddha's teachings, but was concerned that his responsibilities would forever prevent him from following the teachings properly.

Believe it or not, King Suchandra's life was not that different from our own. He had a demanding job (as king), which made him responsible for lots of people (he was under the constant threat of war); he had a wife and kids to provide for and worry about, and he was trying to be a good guy in a world where not everyone was making goodness their top priority. Sound familiar?

So, King Suchandra's question to Buddha is essentially still asked today: 'How can I live like a good and wise person in a world that just doesn't operate that way?'

For me, that translates as, 'How can I live as a peaceful and happy person while living in a culture that operates as a dog-eat-dog, materialist jungle?'

10

NOTICE

Happiness

> When I went to school, they asked me what I
> wanted to be when I grew up. I wrote down 'happy'.
> They told me I didn't understand the assignment,
> and I told them they didn't understand life.
>
> JOHN LENNON

While I'm not sure I believe that five-year-old John Lennon really had the wherewithal to school his teachers in such a profound and philosophical way, I certainly relate to the sentiment. Happiness seems to be largely overlooked as an ambition, and yet it's the one thing every person on the planet wants. Isn't that weird?

Let's go into this with the clear understanding that happiness is impermanent, because we know that's the truth and we know we should always deal with the world as it really is and not how we want it to be. Right? Right. So happiness will never last forever, because nothing does, but neither will unhappiness. Whether we characterise ourselves as happy or unhappy depends on which state we choose to emphasise and on how we choose to interpret our lives.

> Happiness is not something ready-made.
> It comes from your own actions.'
> HIS HOLINESS THE 14TH DALAI LAMA

I used to have a rather unhelpful habit of only acknowledging massive, mind-blowingly awesome moments of happiness. How often do those come along? How often do you accept a proposal, find out you're pregnant, land the job of your dreams, or set foot on the other side of the world for the first time? For most of us, these big moments are few and far between, and our guilty secret is that they're never quite as exciting the second time around.

When we become parents, we try to relive those moments by gifting them to our children. But as anyone who's ever taken a child on a very expensive holiday will tell you, doing so rarely delivers the desired reaction. How could it? I was twenty-seven when I travelled overseas for the first time. I was incredibly excited and grateful for the opportunity. I'd dreamt for months beforehand about what 'overseas' would look, smell and sound like. When I got there (to Scotland, to perform at the Edinburgh Fringe Festival) I couldn't speak for days, I was so overwhelmed by the fact I was there.

When I took my children overseas when they were toddlers, I felt very proud of myself, but now I realise they were never going to get the same buzz I had. Never, ever. It's just baseline for them – because they experienced it so young, it's just part of their normal – which means they'll have to chase something much bigger to get the same feeling of happiness my first trip gave me. Fortunately, Elon Musk's planning to colonise Mars, so there's that for them to aim for, I guess.

I didn't become happier as I ticked items off my wildest-dreams list; instead, I became a greedy, guzzling hungry ghost of a woman. The more big moments I experienced, the more I had to chase get the same high. On top of that, I became temperamental, frazzled and resentful – the complete opposite of who I wanted to be – because it took such an enormous amount of time and energy to make those massive milestones happen.

My ability to notice everyday happiness also slid accordingly. It's very hard to recognise and go with a happy little moment when you're temperamental, frazzled and resentful. Instead, I'd dismiss such moments as worthless wastes of time unless I could see how they might contribute to a massive happiness milestone.

I'd hurry my kids away from piles of autumn leaves, telling them sternly that we didn't have time for playing. Sometimes I'd catch myself later and think, 'What was the hurry, really? I robbed us of a little moment of happiness.'

Very rarely is there actually a need to hurry, but to spend a day with me you'd think I was racing around town saving lives. I'm not, of course, but I developed this intense sense of forward momentum, urging me to get to what's next as quickly as possible. I needed to learn to stop, to give myself a chance to notice moments of happiness. I needed to pay more attention to the experts in the field – children and old people.

Over the last couple of years I've observed that my young children and their aging grandfather have much in common. They all move very slowly and are easily distracted by shiny things and TV commercials. They all rely upon me for transportation and document printing; they all lie about being allowed to drink soft drink, and none of them ever seems to have any money of their own. Nor can they find their own shoes under their beds, but they can all spot an ice-cream shop from the moon.

The other thing they have in common is that happiness visits them many times a day, although rarely as a result of plans I've made for them.

I don't know how many times I've meticulously crafted an outing for my kids in an attempt to bring them joy, only to be rewarded with tears and tantrums because they hated the movie/concert/craft class or whatever. Inevitably, they'll find something of interest as we're leaving, like a drained fountain out front, or a dead possum in the car park. Actually, now that I think about it, the drained fountain and dead possum happened on the same day, and I've never seen them happier.

Similarly, I once drove my father to a local lake and spent twenty minutes setting out chairs, rugs, picnic food and fishing rods, only to turn around and see the unmistakable look of bemused boredom on his face that told me he was ready to go home to his cable TV.

On the way home, even though he's 80 per cent blind, Dad spotted a new waffle café. Suddenly, he wasn't so worried about missing *Duck Dynasty*. Talk about noticing happiness and going with it!

Having twins makes it hard for me to pretend to other mums that outings are going well when they're not. I'm out-numbered by little honesty cops.

'Oh, he loves it!' I'll say to another mum as I'm trying to wrangle my squirming son into an activity. 'No, I don't!' he'll exclaim through gritted teeth.

'He really doesn't, Mum,' his sister will chime in beside us.

Even before they could speak properly they were great communicators. I once took them to a toddlers' music class, and while I sat with my daughter and helped her play a tam-bourine without slashing her face, her brother systematically stole the phones out of every other mother's handbag. At the end of the class I had to pull them out of his pockets and my bag and return them all, as well as hold him back from walking out the door while yelling 'No fank you' to the teacher when she asked if we'd be returning the following week.

We never returned. In fact, we've attended a lot of classes once. There was kinder-gym, at which my daugh-ter almost drowned in a huge foam-filled box. All the other kids did somersaults into the soft landing pit and climbed out beaming, but she sank like a stone and two instructors had to go in after her. We also tried circus school, but when the teacher said my son had to remove his green Crocs, he refused to unlock his arms from around my neck for the entire class. He was so obsessed with those Crocs that he slept in them at night, so the strange lady's lack of respect for them was unforgivable, as far as he was concerned. No. Fank. You.

When we went to see the stage production of *Chitty Chitty Bang Bang*, my daughter was so frightened of the theatre she crapped her dacks, literally, before the curtain went up. Apparently the car flew over the audience just before interval. We'll never know. Those expensive tickets, new outfits, inner-city parking and pre-show lemonades did not add up to happiness.

You know what made my kids happy back then? Playing with clothes pegs in the bath at their nan's, or wandering around the backyard while munching on dog biscuits, or dancing to ads on TV (with Pop telling them to get out of the way so he could see). Sadly, now that they're older, they've fallen into the trap of chasing happiness. They are constantly telling me they'll be happy if they have a certain thing or go to a certain place. Back when they were purer little humans, they didn't engineer happiness. They just wandered through life, making the most of happiness when it happened.

Here's something nice to think about. I'm reasonably confident another little moment of happiness is heading my way, and yours, sooner rather than later. For instance, my kids will arrive home from school soon. They always come giggling loudly up the driveway, calling out the names of the dogs waiting impatiently for them by the kitchen window.

'Hello, Jacko!'

'Hello, Bowie!'

'Have you been good boys today?'

Then they ring the doorbell, the dogs bark, I yell out, 'Who is it?' and they yell back, 'It's us, Mum!' and I'm happy.

Of course, seconds later they'll start fighting over the best biscuits or the last of the Milo and I'll feel lots of other things, but wedged in there will be a moment of real happiness. The trick is noticing it, coming as it does with neither bells nor whistles, nor frequent flyer points.

The challenge is to stop chasing 'unbelievable happiness' and to notice and validate those humble little moments of joy when they present themselves. Surely it's the latter that together make up a life. I'd hate to die waiting for the next moment of unbelievable happiness, always on tiptoe looking up and over all the small moments of happiness falling unnoticed at my feet.

SELF-REFLECTION

Remember a simple moment of happiness from your recent past. Analyse how you responded to it. Did you notice it and suck it in? Or did you shut it down to move on to something 'more important'? You may be lucky like me and know you've got another one coming your way soon. Really commit to it when it arrives, and then make some notes about what you notice. Perhaps it'll be hard to commit to it – perhaps you'll feel a bit silly, or even a bit bored. Just make sure you really connect with your feelings and give yourself a chance to work through them later.

Sometimes, connecting with our true feelings can be tricky. After some self-reflection, I realised that there are times when I feel too vulnerable to really engage with reality and be happy. I hold back and play it cool, usually because of trust issues with someone involved, like my ex-husband or my father. Over the years, both have made me feel pretty silly on occasion for loving them. I worry that if they know I'm happy, they'll turn on me! Intellectually I know that's unfair, and it's a big emotional overreaction, but it's hard to get past sometimes. I'm telling you this because I want you to be honest with yourself about your feelings, even if they make you blush!

11

ADD

Some Stuff

Life cannot only be made up of things that are important to the bigger picture. As we've discussed, there's no guarantee the big picture will be as big as we're hoping. There's no guarantee the restful future of earned enjoyment will actually happen, so some stuff has to be done purely for the joy it brings us right here, right now.

Once every couple of months or so, I have a Saturday night out with friends. We call it a book club, but very little literary material is discussed. It's really just an excuse for a couple of mums to go out to a cheap local restaurant and have a few drinks and a laugh. Socialising with women who also have young kids is great because we all want the evening to begin and end early. Usually, we're tucked up in our own beds, slightly sozzled, by 11 p.m. Perfect.

As much as I look forward to these nights, when the day rolls around I often regret saying yes. I'm invariably tired, with a sink full of dishes, a laundry full of dirty clothes, a column or podcast that needs finishing and a Netflix series calling my name. As the hour of the outing draws near, and I start to think about getting dressed and putting make-up on, cancellation fantasies flash through my mind with increasing frequency, and I often give in to them. When I don't, though, when I actually push myself into the shower, into some clothes and into the car, I'm always happy I did.

Yes, there are more productive things I could do with that time; yes, social engagements are just more dots in the diary that feel like lead weights around my neck when I open it up; and yes, having a quiet night at home in tracky dacks helps to alleviate the crushing feeling of unbelievable busy-ness. However, socialising makes me feel more like a person and less like a machine built to service others. I consider it an act of self-care.

I sometimes think that the only avoidable things in my life, the only things I can say no to, are things for myself. Activities that benefit only me seem the most expendable, but that attitude leaves me feeling overburdened and resentful, and my busyness feels like an inescapable hell of my own making.

You can't pour from an empty cup.

ANON

Self-care is very important to Buddhists because we believe that generosity is a crucial ingredient in a happy life. How can I be generous if I feel drained? How can I give to others if I don't also give to myself? If I wish to lead a long life of generosity, I must nurture myself as well.

Certainly, there have been times – those crying in the shower moments, for example – when I've felt as though I had nothing left to give my children. There have been nights when I've seriously thought about getting up, walking out of the house, getting into my car and just going. I didn't know where – just somewhere quiet where I could be alone. I felt desperately empty in those moments.

Those moments were caused by my failure to care enough for myself. I'd allowed myself to become completely drained, when at the very least I still needed to have enough energy to look after my children. Giving everything we have isn't wise, or even generous in the long term, because it means we'll have to stop altogether at some point. We will literally run out. I needed a realistic program of self-care, one that helped me fill up on a daily basis, to live the happy, generous life I wanted to.

WISDOM AND COMPASSION

This brings us to Buddha's famous teachings about wisdom and compassion, two sides of the one coin. While compassion is wonderful and important if we want to be happy, without wisdom it can easily spin out of control and create problems. Just ask my ex-husband, who so often had to provide the wisdom to my compassion. For many years I thought that giving away everything I had, from possessions and money to my time and energy, was the way to follow Buddha's teachings and obtain happiness. While giving does make me happy, it has also been known to make me broke and exhausted. Being broke and exhausted means I can't keep giving.

My compassion without wisdom meant that not only was my family broke sometimes, but we tended to have lots of responsibilities. At any given moment we might've had a handful of geriatric (and incontinent) dogs I was trying to shepherd towards peaceful deaths; injured mice I'd rescued from the cat; a litter of abandoned kittens in the spare room, awaiting their forever homes; foster children around the globe requiring regular cash; and a heavy hand when it came to a donation jar. Most of the actual hands-on caring for the menagerie fell to my husband, because I was out working or volunteering, or bringing another random animal home. That poor man. Do you now see why he divorced me?

My excessive compassion really started to get out of hand in the early days of my Buddhism. 'A little knowledge is a dangerous thing,' so they say, and I definitely went hard at Buddhism with very little understanding of how all the teachings connect.

It came to a head when I rescued a little dog, then had to have him euthanised. He was so territorial he dug out of our backyard and bit several of our neighbours in their own yards. Though he was a beautiful little fellow at home, something had happened before we adopted him that confused him and made him dangerous. After a couple of years and a couple of thousand dollars on fences and trainers, I had to let him go. It was one of the most traumatic events of my life. I've rescued a lot of animals in my time, and never, ever had to give up on one. I felt like I'd failed him so badly. It still breaks my heart to think about that little dog.

On a spiritual level, I felt totally confused. I didn't understand how such good intentions could've turned out so badly. When I went to see a local Geshe – a Buddhist monk of high standing, kind of like a professor of Buddhism – he set me the task of reading and thinking about wisdom and compassion, and how important they are to each other.

It really helped me a lot and gradually, over the next couple of years, as our geriatric and injured animal friends passed away, I was able to resist the urge to replace them. I reduced my day-to-day responsibilities to a more manageable level, and I slowly lowered the financial donations I was making, so that I could get my finances under control and commit to donating less but for longer. I'd turned a blind eye to the chaos I'd been living in and perpetuating, but once it started to dissipate, I had to admit it felt really good. I felt like I could actually breathe again.

I still adopt abandoned animals but I have a strict one in, one out policy. We don't adopt a new pet until the current one has passed away, and we don't take on any animals with behavioural difficulties because I've accepted I'm not Cesar Millan the Dog Whisperer. So disappointed about that.

Of course, having pets is definitely part of my self-care. As a child, I'd curl up on the couch with my little sausage dog, Cindy, for at least an hour every day. We'd look lovingly into each other's eyes, and I'd gently stroke the bridge of her nose and between her eyes, and run her soft ears between my fingers while having one of those pretend conversations about what a clever dog she was and what plans she had for the day. It's pretty much the same ritual I'll perform tonight with my cattle dog, Jacko, only we'll have a couple of squabbling children banging into us intermittently to contend with. It's still good, though.

Spending time with animals really recharges me; I just have to remember to balance compassion with wisdom and stay on the middle path, like with everything else, not pushing it to the point where it becomes too draining.

So, let's now create space for some serious self-care.

SELF-REFLECTION

Cast an eye over your house and your life and work out what (or who) drains you most. Write a list in your journal. Once you've identified them, see if there are any you can let go of. I'm serious now – this is how I decided to get divorced, so I'm not playing around here. I want you to be very strong about this. Is there anything that's emptying you that you can get rid of, and take that pressure off your life?

- Is there a relationship that drains rather than nourishes you?

- Are there people living in your home who are old enough to be living in their own place?

- Do you have unnecessary financial burdens? This includes financial goals – once you've really unpicked them, you might find there's a lot of ego and not a lot of sense behind them. Do your kids really have to go to that posh school? Do you really need that flash car, or to live in that expensive neighbourhood? How hard are you working just for the ego trip of accumulating trophies for others to admire?

12

TURN ON ALL YOUR

Burners

Have you ever heard of the Four Burners Theory? I heard it mentioned offhand in a podcast a couple of months ago, which made me think I must be the only person who doesn't know about it. If you don't either, then allow me to bring you up to speed, because I find it really fascinating and helpful, and I reckon you might too.

The Four Burners Theory is really just a fresh take on that old chestnut, work-life balance. The idea is that you divide up your life into four categories: family, friends, health and work. Now, picture each of those categories as a burner on a cooktop. Next, imagine turning all four burners on and watching them glowing brightly. Sounds pretty good, right? Like that's the recipe for a full and happy life?

Here's the kicker, though: to be *successful* – in our Western sense of the word – you have to turn off one of the burners. And what's worse, in order to be super-duper successful, you have to turn off *two* of them.

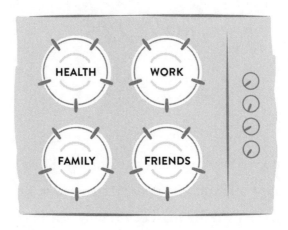

This theory blew my mind. It was suddenly so clear to me that I'd cut off my friends and health burners long ago. To be honest, I cut off my family burner right up until Adrian and I decided to have kids. At that time, I did at least have my health burner on a bit. I exercised every day and ate well; in fact, in 2007 I decided I wanted to be a person who ran, so I gradually worked at it until I could run an hour without stopping. That was massive for me, having given up on running at a young age because I was so slow and teased for it, by kids and teachers alike. Back then I decided I was a person who didn't run, but at thirty-five I changed that. It was a wonderful bit of Shoshin, if I do say so myself, and I'd like to think I'll get it back one day. (At the moment, I just can't imagine spending an hour a day on exercise. I am exercising semi-regularly again, but I must admit, if I get time to myself all I can think of is lying down.)

As a woman in my mid-forties, my body has given me lots of signs over the last few years that things are changing again. As comedian Judith Lucy once said, 'Who knew tweezers would become such an important part of life after forty?' It's yet another time in my life when I find myself thinking, 'Oh no, is it really that time already?' I remember having that thought when I started getting boobs, and it feels like I've had a dreadful realisation about my body every couple of years since then, up to and including my first long, strong grey hair about six months ago. It was particularly startling, sprouting as it did in the space between my aforementioned boobs. *Wow. Is it really that time already?* Yes, it seems it is.

I realised when I started to suffer crippling pain in my left hip after a lap of my local supermarket that I was in danger of turning into a particular type of middle-aged woman – one who turns into an immobile old woman. In my mind, I'm still twenty-six, of course, buzzing around the place in a body that's overweight but fit and strong. In reality, my skeleton was starting to hurt. I decided to undergo weight loss surgery (gastric bypass) in late 2016, and I'm so glad I did. Yes, it's embarrassing to have to go to that length to rein my body in, but I'd rather be embarrassed than unable to walk. In a way I feel lucky to have had such clear signals from my body that I needed to turn my health burner back on, when I still had time to do something about it.

When I first heard the Four Burners Theory, I realised that my friends burner needed to be switched back on too. For a long time I thought that working in such a social industry, with lots of people I call friends, meant that going out after hours was a 'waste' of time. However, I've come to realise that the conversations are much more meaningful when we're not trying to fit them in around work. When we're not constantly being interrupted or needing to talk in code about private stuff, we can get to much deeper places, in which I really feel like I'm benefitting from the insights of others. I decided that the bi-monthly night out with my so-called book club wasn't cutting it, and I've since made a concerted effort to more regularly catch up with friends. It doesn't have to be a big deal; in fact, the smaller the better, as far as I'm concerned. Meeting another mum from school an hour before pick-up is a good one, or a weekend meet-up for a cheap meal somewhere kid-friendly. We've got to feed them, right? Why not combine a few families and do the job together? I have a friend who does 'pancake Sunday' once a month at her place. She just sends a message to her Whats-App group a few days before to remind them it's on, and then they roll over whenever they're ready, possibly still in PJs, for a relaxing breakfast of pancakes and coffee. All the grown-ups chip in, so it's not a lot of work and it ensures the friends of all ages connect with each other regularly. That lady has four kids and a demanding job, and her husband owns a business, but her friends burner is red hot.

Turning up your friends burner can also help ease your sense of being unbelievably busy if you're honest with friends you trust about your problems. One of our most self-destructive habits is assuming no-one else will under-stand our struggles. I hate to say it, but we have a tendency to think we are special and unique. One of my delusions holding me back was the idea that I was burdening other people by telling them my problems. When I sat quietly for long enough and really thought about it, though, I realised it was more a case of me not wanting to admit I was failing or feeling vulnerable. It was just a good old-fashioned trust issue. I didn't trust people to still want me around if I was complaining.

When we open up to others, though, and engage with them honestly, instead of trying to look perfect all the time, we'll usually find someone who understands what we're going through because they're experiencing the same things themselves (or have done in the past). As Nikki did with her neighbour Trish, we then relax about our problems because we can see they're not bizarre or remarkable. Our friends can often give us practical advice or help, or even just some comfort by reminding us that all difficulties eventually pass. At some point, teenage girls are released by their hormones and self-obsession, teenage boys lose their aversion to the shower, and I'm hoping that little boys learn to flush the toilet, too. Don't forget, everything and everyone is always changing – try to find someone who's good at reminding you of that fact when you really need to hear it.

No human can survive without help. We are designed to work together in societies. Bear that in mind when you are struggling, and have the humility to ask for help. I've found that reaching out to others at my lowest points and being honest about what a mess I'm in is how I've found my best friends. I know these people don't want to hang out with me because they believe in some false image my ego has created. They are attracted to me because they're open-hearted and real. Does it get any better than that when it comes to forming a #squad?

13

CREATE

So here I am, complaining on the one hand about being unbelievably busy, and on the other trying to think of more things to do. Obviously, getting all four burners going at once is a real juggle, and takes some serious prioritising. I have one suggestion as to how to get started, which helped me a lot: fight for your right to a weekend.

When I was younger I worked weekends, either performing or in hospitality of some kind. When I no longer had to work weekends, I automatically filled them up with work-like things: I volunteered, I helped out with worthy causes, I signed my kids up for stuff I thought would stimulate their minds, etc. I guess it was because of my fear of an unproductive moment. I just saw two empty days and sought to fill them with purpose. I now believe with all my heart that was a mistake. I believe in weekends!

There's a lot of talk these days about the benefits of letting our children experience boredom. Experts say boredom encourages kids to explore and create, and that if we fill up all their time we're robbing them of the opportunity to utilise and expand their imaginations, not to mention just navel-gaze. Would I have spent so much time as a kid stroking my dog's face on the couch if I'd had an iPad and an Xbox? Would I still have chosen to stare into her eyes and think about the world and our place in it?

I think adults are also terrified of boredom. My ex-husband, for all his relaxed wisdom, cannot stand a quiet house. I know for a fact that right now, as you're reading this, he'll have a TV and two radios on all at once. One radio is in the kitchen, the other in the bedroom and the TV is in the lounge room, so there isn't a quiet corner in the place. It drove me crazy when we lived together, and the minute he'd go out, I'd turn them all off and bathe in the silence. As soon as he'd walk back in, he'd say, 'God, it's so quiet!' and switch them all back on again. He's quite conscious of why he 'needs' noise. He says that silence gives him a 'busy head'. He is trying to protect himself from his own thoughts.

Similarly, I built a wall of activity to protect myself, no doubt about it. By carving a big, gaping hole in it for weekends, I was forced to face myself in a really significant way. I first made a concerted effort to keep Sundays free, and then I expanded it to the entire weekend. No work of any kind – including writing, catching up on the week's emails, etc. – and no big working bees around the house. Early on there were days when I felt so lost I'd seriously start thinking about painting a room, or buying a flat pack to assemble – and I really hate flat packs! But I knew it was busy work, designed to protect me from my own thoughts, and it defeated the purpose. Now, I allow myself to potter about the house, maybe move a few things around, but no massive two-day projects to keep me unbelievably busy.

I also don't do any volunteering or charity events on weekends anymore. I know that seems harsh but, as we learnt earlier, an empty cup cannot pour. This will seem harsh too: no social events that don't really interest me. Now I ask myself, 'Will that event nourish me or will it drain me?' The answer determines whether I'll accept or decline the invitation. It's that simple.

For two days a week, I'm not that unbelievably busy person rushing to whatever's next. So, who am I? This is what I mean by facing myself. There are moments now, as I wander around my quiet house in my socks, with a treatment in my hair, sipping a cup of tea and checking on dinner in the slow cooker, when I actually feel I'm the person I want to be.

I'm also much more generous on weekends. It's strange but I say things like, 'It's okay, I'm not in a hurry,' when the barista at the cafe apologises for the wait. It's weirdly empowering to be able to stop and wave other drivers into my lane because I'm not running late. I'm not chasing anything, so I have the time and mental space to notice happiness on the weekends, and it makes me want more of it.

No is a complete sentence.

UNKNOWN

To prioritise, it's also essential to learn how to say no. When pop star Kesha asked Jerry Seinfeld for a hug while they were mingling on the red carpet, he didn't hesitate to look her in the eye and say, 'No.' It was such a strange moment that she asked again. Again, he said simply, 'No, no thanks.'

Jerry has never struck me as a big hugger, and he explained later that he just isn't into hugging strangers. This is perfectly reasonable, but usually we comply with this request whether we're into it or not, because to say 'no' to someone when put on the spot like that is incredibly difficult. We often coax our children into hugging people they don't want to, while at the same time warning them about protecting their personal space from people who want to touch them. It's all very confusing. No wonder as adults we find it easier to submit to awkward requests than to simply say, 'No, no thanks.'

People I've worked with will tell you I have no trouble saying 'no'. In recent years I've added 'mate' – as in, 'No, mate' – to soften the blow and make it more friendly, because I was often saying it to people I liked and enjoyed working with. Radio shows revolve around a constant flow of ideas, from a pool of up to a dozen people, but my attitude was that as long as my name was on the show, I needed to be comfortable with an idea for it to make it on air. If I didn't like it, for whatever reason, I had to be able to say, 'No, mate.'

In other aspects of my life, though, I was as no-phobic as anyone. That's why I became such a prolific liar. Anyone who gets up before dawn for work will tell you that it creates a kind of tiredness that can't be shaken off for the weekend, or simply ignored for a good cause. Saying 'no' to lovely people because you're too exhausted to go to their party is the worst. Probably not for Jerry Seinfeld, but it was for me, so I got into the habit of lying about why I couldn't go, or sometimes I would say I'd go if I thought they wouldn't notice a no-show. I'm not proud of it, but it was a coping mechanism and I had no trouble sleeping at night, knowing I hadn't stolen any valuable sleeping time from myself.

14

PRIORITISE

I used to find it hard to relax until my to-do list was completed. That I got from my mamma. 'Ah, just do it tomorrow,' my ex-husband would say, trying to be helpful.

'But that'll make tomorrow's list even longer,' I'd reply, eyebrows raised, insinuating he was being insensitive about my workload.

That all changed when my twins were newborns and needed to be fed every three hours. It took approximately two-and-a-half hours to feed, burp and change them both. Yes, you read that right: we had half an hour between feeds. I never figured out how to breastfeed one kid properly, let alone both at once like you see in pictures online, so I expressed milk into bottles and used formula for the shortfall.

Initially I tried to get everything done before I had a sleep, like sterilising the bottles, making a jug of formula, throwing baby clothes in the washing machine, throwing my own body into some kind of washing arrangement, feeding myself, etc., etc., etc. As usual, their father would say, 'Why don't you just do that later?' Unusually, I finally took his advice. I left some of the jobs for the 2 a.m. shift, which was completely unintuitive for me, but it worked.

For the first time in my life I realised the importance of rest. I couldn't kid myself that I could keep going, or that completing a to-do list was the most beneficial use of my time. I understood that in order to get through that list at all, I had to be the boss of it, rather than allow it to be the boss of me. Sometimes, rest had to move to the top of the list. Previously, I'd always thought of rest as a reward, an indulgence that was allowed only after every single thing that could be done had been done. That's so stupid, isn't it? Have a wild guess where I got that from.

I remember one Christmas when my father worked thirty-six hours – straight. It's a lucrative time for cabs because lots of people are out drinking, all day and all night, from Christmas Eve until Boxing Day, moving between their homes, relatives' homes and local pubs. Some taxi drivers choose to have the big day itself off to spend with their families, if you can believe that. My father certainly couldn't, and he was thrilled to be one of the few taxis on the road during that busy time.

That was the time Dad's mate gave him some tiny pills to help him through. Out he went at about 7 p.m. Christmas Eve, only returning when the last reveller had been delivered home as the sun rose on Boxing Day. This achievement was entered into legend in our family, and Dad's blind eyes still twinkle when it's mentioned.

I guess that's why I felt a bit soft about having a nap between newborn twin feeds. It could also explain my nonchalance about using little pills to get me through.

Now I understand that pushing myself when I'm exhausted often means I'll take longer to do a job, and I'll do it shabbily. If I put it off until I've had some rest, chances are I'll get it done faster and with less crying and swearing. (Not only do my kids find the crying and swearing scary, it also makes it hard for me to chastise them when they do the same.)

Rest is crucial – we know that. Sleep deprivation is a form of torture banned under the Geneva Convention, and yet we're too shy to fight for our right to sleep. This might be justified, in a way – I know of a very experienced radio performer who was sacked because she'd lie on the studio floor during songs. She was in her fifties and had been working those hideous breakfast hours for over twenty years, while also raising her sons. All her boss could say for years afterwards was, 'She was lying on the floor!'

A younger, more energetic model was brought in with zero impact on the show's ratings, but we all learnt our lesson. Exhaustion was unacceptable. The fact that the boss was a woman of similar age and circumstances highlights the lack of tolerance for human frailty in our success-driven modern workplaces.

Despite this, if we want to have more fulfilling lives, with time for peace, rest and small moments of happiness, we have to create space. Obviously we can't let go of all our responsibilities, and a life of nothing *but* rest would be just as unfulfilling as a life of total busyness. It's about balance.

15

PRIORITISE

Peace

THROUGH DAILY PRACTICE

Buddhists believe that there's a big difference between rest and peace. Rest happens when you do nothing, and you can rest without having peace. You might rest better if you are peaceful, but one is a state of being and one is simply an activity. Peace is a much higher goal than rest, and much harder to achieve. It takes a lot of work.

Peace doesn't just come to you – well, not in a sustained way, anyway. Though every now and then we do stumble upon a little bit of peace, don't we? Just last night I found myself in my freshly made bed with no-one other than my dog, Jacko. Usually both kids and their little dog are squirming around in there too, fighting over what to watch on TV. But last night it was just me and my hairy, farty man.

It was a chilly night but my clean sheets were flannelette, as were my clean jim jams, and I was ever so cosy. I grabbed the remote and searched the 'Meshel' section of Netflix – you know, where it tells you what you'll like because you've watched other stuff? It's a rare honour to have the time to scroll around that section, and happily I found *Grace and Frankie*, the sitcom featuring Lily Tomlin and Jane Fonda. As the theme song played, I kissed Jacko on the head and said, 'How peaceful is this, big boy?'

He licked my face, farted and sighed before curling up under my arm. It was bliss.

So the question is, how do I have that wonderful feeling more often? The answer, I believe, is by creating spaces for it to happen, and through daily practice of mindfulness, meditation and setting intentions.

A great way to begin changing your life (aside from reading this book, of course) is to start meditating. It's not easy to break old habits and well-established thought patterns, but the first step is mindfulness – being present with your thoughts and feelings, so you can really deal with them. Mindfulness means connecting with what we're actually feeling and thinking, and calmly and rationally exploring them.

We can do everything we normally do mindfully. We can eat mindfully, walk mindfully and even rest mindfully. We just need to train ourselves to focus on the moment we are in. Next time you have the opportunity to eat alone, try doing it without any other distractions. Don't turn on the TV or grab a magazine or your phone. Don't grab a pen and paper to write a list of things you have to do later. In fact, don't think about anything in the past or the future – just think about exactly what you are doing in that moment.

Concentrate on chewing and the flavours of the food, because when you're mindful, you realise there are many flavours all at once, not just one. My mum's lasagne doesn't taste like 'lasagne'. It tastes of sweet tomato, and salty cheese, of peppery bechamel sauce and the deep, red-wine caramel of the meat. I didn't notice those flavours until very recently, even though I'd been eating Mum's lasagne for forty years.

When attempting to eat mindfully, focus on the food in your mouth. Feel the way your tongue expertly moves it around your teeth, and how your teeth grind and mash it until it's smooth. Feel it move gently down your throat, maybe aided by a sip of water, and listen to the gurgles the process produces.

Take your time and complete every mouthful before loading your fork with the next one. Feel the fork as it digs through the food on your plate, and heaves with the food. Feel the metal slide gracefully between your teeth. Feel your stomach fill.

By practising mindfulness in very simple daily tasks, we can develop the ability to listen to ourselves, which is something few of us are really able to do, and to pull ourselves into our own singular experience. We can be surrounded by thousands of people, but no two people are experiencing the situation in exactly the same way. Our experience is always personal.

Mindfulness helps us to create mental space for ourselves, no matter what's going on around us. I've developed the ability to sort of stand outside chaotic situations, and to think clearly (and quickly) about my best course of action before stepping back in. This is a very handy skill in live television and radio! I can sometimes be interviewing someone who is raving on and on without taking a breath, while someone else is yelling in my earpiece to wrap it up because the ads are late and all hell's about to break loose in the control room.

Rather than losing myself in either one of the experiences I'm in the middle of, I can calmly isolate myself for a second (while actually staying exactly where I am physically) to make a decision. I might realise in that second that the storyteller seems to be reaching a natural conclusion, in which case I need to prepare myself to laugh heartily, thank them quickly and get to the ads. I might realise they are just moving from topic to topic with no point whatsoever, in which case I need to think of a cheerful, gracious way to say we've unfortunately run out of time, and thank them quickly before getting to the ads.

Mindfulness is also handy when I find myself caught in the middle of a heated battle between my kids. It's always over something really important, like whose turn it is to sit in the front seat or something. Both are unequivocal it's their turn, both beg me to intercede on their behalf, and neither realises how little I care. The drama intensifies until I want to shove them both to the ground to give me a head start as I run away. Instead, I try to engage my ninja mindfulness powers of isolating myself so I can make a logical decision. It's generally a case of figuring out who I can blackmail or buy off the quickest, with the threat of a cancelled play date or a Shopkins car – because, let's be honest, there's really no way of knowing whose turn it really is. The truth is not the answer, in this particular case; the fighting just needs to stop.

Getting caught up in other people's stress just makes it that much harder for me to be helpful in any way. Isolating myself through mindfulness enables me to decide for myself how I want to proceed. The alternative is to react in the moment and regret it later. 'Act in haste, repent at leisure,' as my old granny used to say.

Meditation is the next step in our training to isolate ourselves. Even without eating or walking to concentrate on, we listen to our bodies, our own life force, as we focus on the breath moving in and out. Later, whenever thoughts creep into our minds, we go back to listening to the breath. It's about pulling ourselves out of the matrix of distractions so we can think clearly.

For years I meditated in my car before going into work in the morning. It was a quick five-minute job, and it definitely helped me go inside with a reasonably positive attitude most days. More recently, as I worked on overcoming my unbelievable busyness, I realised it was time to step it up. It was time to prioritise meditation.

If you've ever come along to hear me speak about Buddhism, you'll know that I like to begin the sessions with a guided meditation. There are many reasons for this: it helps get people settled and leave whatever else is going on in their lives behind for a little while, it encourages us all to get into a spiritual headspace, and it gets us to listen to ourselves, which we so rarely do.

When we meditate, first we simply listen to our breath moving in and out of our bodies. Then we focus more specifically on feeling it move over our lips and up our noses, and down our throats until it expands our chests. We take note of what parts of our bodies move to allow that air in, and then of what our body does when the air is breathed out again.

Just following that pattern for a time, and returning to it whenever our minds wander, helps us to recognise all of the things we're made up of. We can feel and hear our very organs going about their business. It places us in the present moment, clears our heads, and reminds us that everything in our body is connected, which is the way of the world too.

We've talked about the many ways we distract ourselves, and meditation seems scary because it's the opposite of that. I dread it sometimes, usually because I just want to be engrossed by something shiny on my phone. But as soon as I drop down into those deep breaths, it feels relaxing, and I'm glad I did. There's something so good about taking time to sit and listen to your own body – it makes you feel like you're caring for yourself, and that affects the way you walk out into the world.

A slightly different but very simple and gentle kind of meditation you can try is a tea meditation. It reminds me of the prayer of grace we used to chant at my Catholic high school: 'Bless us, oh Lord, and these, thy gifts, which we are about to receive, through Christ our Lord, Amen.' That's a mouthful, and I never really put too much thought into it as a kid, but as an adult I can see how valuable it is to take the time to acknowledge the simple joy of eating and drinking.

The beautiful Vietnamese monk Thich Nhat Hanh champions a tea meditation. He describes it like this:

You must be completely awake in the present to enjoy the tea.

Only in the awareness of the present, can your hands

feel the pleasant warmth of the cup.

Only in the present, can you savor the aroma, taste the sweetness, appreciate the delicacy.

If you are ruminating about the past, or worrying about the future, you will completely miss the experience of enjoying the cup of tea.

You will look down at the cup, and the tea will be gone.

Life is like that.

If you are not fully present, you will look around and it will be gone.

You will have missed the feel, the aroma, the delicacy and beauty of life.

It will seem to be speeding past you. The past is finished.

Learn from it and let it go.

The future is not even here yet. Plan for it, but do not waste your time worrying about it.

Worrying is worthless.

When you stop ruminating about what has already

happened, when you stop worrying about what might never happen, then you will be in the present moment.

Then you will begin to experience joy in life.

I encourage you to stick these beautiful words somewhere you can read them while holding a cup of tea. The next time you're feeling stressed and overwhelmed, take just ten minutes or so to sip some lovely warm tea while reading Thich Nhat Hanh's meditation. Trust me, you won't regret it.

As well as meditation, the Buddhist practice of setting daily intentions will help you stay focused on your goal of long-term change. Be clear about how you want to be in the world, and remind yourself of it every morning. As an example, you could say out loud to yourself something like, 'My intention today is to notice small moments of happiness.' By placing this idea in the forefront of your mind, you're more likely to remember it throughout the day, especially when you most need it.

Mindfulness will help you notice all of those things to be grateful for. It's really amazing how we can take the same trip in a different mindset and have a totally different experience. Try staying completely in the moment on your daily commute to work, the one you've done a thousand times. Don't block it out with electronics, or even a book. Really experience every moment. Smell the air as you walk to the train or the car, and feel it on your skin. Is it hot or cold? Are there flowers or animals along your path? Take them in. Hear the birds. Absorb the scenery, smile at children and dogs, press your palms together and feel your own body heat. Notice as much of this life of yours as you can, because it won't always exist. You may yearn for these memories one day.

16

BEWARE THE PERILS OF

Social Media

Another way to create way more space in your life – not only in terms of time, but also headspace – is to spend less time on social media.

Never before have so many people been so addicted to something they agree is problematic. We blame social media for everything, from the lack of sex in relationships to the rise in narcissism. Actually, maybe that's not such a broad spectrum: it's not easy to make love to someone when you're busy loving yourself sick and obsessively checking the likes on your photoshopped selfies.

Life has certainly become more demanding since our 'social' life became a 24-hour proposition. There was a time not too long ago when we'd retreat to our own private space at the end of the day. We'd take off our make-up and pull on our most hideous clothes because no-one was going to see us but our family, our lover and/or our housemate, all of whom were hideous and relaxed as well. Then we'd sit and watch tele, chatting with whomever happened to be home. If we didn't much like the person on tele, we'd talk about it but just to each other. Yes, kids, it was like real-life Gogglebox.

We didn't attempt to track down the contact details of the TV person so we could tell them our judgement of their performance, their character or their appearance. No, we were content to simply agree with whoever was beside us that she was a stuck-up, fat moll, or that he thought he was hot shit, and then we went to bed.

In those days, our social performance was done for the day once we'd got home and closed the front door behind us, and we had around twelve hours to recharge and regroup before facing the world again. It seems incredibly balanced in retrospect, but it's just not the case anymore.

Now we're expected to keep our social game faces on all night as friends, acquaintances and total randoms engage with us online – sometimes playfully, sometimes not. We have to be ready for whatever is thrown at us, and it seems like no matter how hard we try to keep it breezy and non-controversial, someone somewhere will give us feedback – even some KPIs – regarding our appearance, or our parenting, or whatever else they think we're doing wrong.

It's so exhausting, isn't it? And though we're alert and alarmed about the effects of social media bullying on children and young adults, we're not as careful and protective of ourselves. Most of my friends who have children older than mine confiscate electronics at night to prevent the youngsters from engaging in social media when they should be sleeping, but they don't set a cut-off time for themselves.

I must admit, I look forward to indulging in late-night socials once my kids have finally dropped off to sleep. It's like a last tiny island of adult time for the day, after hours of post-school kid stuff. By this time, I'm usually craving some headlines, of both the news and social media varieties. I want to know about any and all interesting developments in the government, my neighbourhood, my network of high-school friends, and Brad and Angie's custody arrangements that have happened since I picked up my kids at 3.15 p.m., please! And don't spare the clickbait and outrage!

Not only that, don't just tell me what's happened – please tell me what everyone thinks about it too, so I can quickly figure out what I think and then move on to the next story. It's very convenient for a busy working mum like myself.

A shark attack off a beach? They should cull all the sharks! A pop star has died? Who cares, you didn't even know them! They want to build a prison in a nearby suburb? Well, they have to build it somewhere! The baby of an old friend from uni ate a snail? Kids can die from eating snails, you terrible mother!

Suddenly, it's on for young and old and I'm lying in bed, clutching my phone with my heart racing and my eyes widening like I'm in the middle of some bizarre, overfamiliar, philosophical pub brawl. It's not relaxing, and it often keeps me awake until long after I wanted to be asleep. In fact, even though I spend all day fantasising about sleep, I constantly waste precious sleeping time by scrolling on my phone as it shoots bright white light into my eyeballs and brain.

On the other hand, there have been periods in my life when if it weren't for social media I'd have had no social life at all. When I didn't have the time, energy or cash to actually go out and see my friends, or even just speak on the phone, sometimes a direct message, a comment or even just a 'like' was the only evidence I could give them that I was still alive!

As my long-time friends and I have grown older, moved around and had kids, our socials have allowed us to stay connected. Some might say it's an inauthentic connection because everyone lies on social media, but I don't believe that. I still know lots of details, big and small, about my friend Cassandra's life, despite the fact we haven't been in the same room in over a decade. I've watched her children grow from toddlers on remote beaches in Far North Queensland to preschoolers in the Bavarian snow and now to primary-schoolers in the NSW rainforest.

I remember being confused as a kid when my mum would stumble across old photos and say the smiling characters in them were people she 'used to know'. *You either know them or you don't*, I used to think, but I get it now. Life changes constantly and completely. If it weren't for good old Facey, Cassandra would be someone I used to know but, wonderfully, I still get to call her my friend.

Of course, not everyone is honest on social media. It's funny how we all say we have a friend who lies about their life being better than it really is on socials, but none of us ever admits to doing it. I'm not exactly the #blessed type, by which I mean I don't use my social media feeds to create a false impression of myself as perfect, with perfect kids and a perfectly clean, sunlit house. I'm sad to say I'm not constantly #grateful, and I'm not organised enough to make it look like I am. As much as I try to keep it real, though, I'll definitely reframe a cute photo of my kids to cut out a recycling bin overflowing with pizza boxes in the background.

If you are lying about your life on social media – like, a lot – I'm not going to ask you to come out of your dirty closet and confess you're not as happy, or tidy, or grateful as you pretend. However, I will ask you to think about why you lie. Do you want others to feel envious of you? Do you feel that way about your friends? Are you ashamed of your real life? How much time are you wasting creating this idealised version of your life? Lastly, is it an avoidable element of your unbelievably busy life?

Even if you never post anything yourself, social media can create problems by providing a deep dark cave to hide in. It's one of the ways in which we can remove ourselves from our real lives and the present. I can spend hours flicking between Facebook, Twitter, Instagram, email and my favourite news sites – just flicking, flicking, flicking. Occasionally, I'm embarrassed to admit, I'm well aware I'm avoiding interacting with people, even my children, by burying myself in my phone.

Sometimes I'm waiting for something interesting to pop up, but sometimes I know it's the flipping itself that I'm addicted to. There's no doubt that our phones and their apps are engineered to trigger addictive levers in our brains. Tristan Harris is a former 'product philosopher' for Google. (Don't you just love a good hipster Silicon Valley job title?) Anyway, he co-funded Time Well Spent, an advocacy group trying to bring moral integrity to software design, and to persuade the tech world to help us disengage more easily from our devices.

'You could say that it's [your] responsibility' to exercise self-control when it comes to digital usage, he explains, 'but that's not acknowledging that there's a thousand people on the other side of the screen whose job is to break down whatever responsibility [you] can maintain.'

The more time we spend scrolling, the more likely we are to click on an ad, buy another app and give away more of our personal information, which will be sold to companies that want us to keep scrolling. We're also more likely to inadvertently subscribe to a mailing list, giving us even more emails to delete every day and thereby adding to our unbelievable busyness.

One of the many disadvantages of our love affair with social media is that it enables us to see the world as we want to see it, rather than how it really is. This phenomenon is called 'confirmation bias', and it's defined on Wikipedia as 'the tendency to interpret new evidence as confirmation of one's existing beliefs and theories'. My friends and I call it 'the bubble', and we talk openly about retreating to it when the real world gets too contrary for us.

Here's how our bubbles are created. When we join groups and like articles on Facebook, algorithms designed to keep us on Facebook for as long as possible then send us more and more stuff along the lines of what we've already liked and joined. Before we know it, our feeds are full of posts agreeing with us and proving we are right about everything. Why would we look for other news sources when our Facebook feed is conveniently full of breaking news told from our own biased perspectives? This is how my mother and I can have completely conflicting understandings of the same news story, both believing some degree of 'alternative facts'.

However, when I've tried to keep my sources of information many and varied, I've felt like I've been stumbling from one dramatic debate to another, if not participating then at least witnessing and emotionally investing. From climate change to marriage equality to immigration, to the naming of celebrity babies and whether or not pubes should be allowed to exist, it seems that everyone has a strong opinion based on personal insight which NEEDS TO BE WRITTEN IN CAPS AND OVERLY PUNCTUATED!!!!!!

It was overwhelming, time-consuming and draining, and would lead me straight back to my bubble. I'd retreat from reality again, scrolling, scrolling, scrolling through my Facebook feed full of posts that make me feel right and noble. This is a big no no for a Buddhist. As we know, Buddha taught us to engage with the world as it really is and not as we wish it to be.

> Social media is arguably the greatest source affecting our arising today. It's sculpted so neatly around our existing perceptions and biases that it's stunting us and preventing us from growing outward. That detracts from our quality of life.

I couldn't change the fact that social media is now a pervasive cultural force, and I don't really know what an algorithm is, so I couldn't change any of those. I could only change myself.

Gandhi, the great Hindu leader of Indian independence and the peaceful protest movement, was pretty good on this topic. He said, 'Be the change you wish to see in the world.'

The change I wanted to see in the world was more engagement with reality, and greater emphasis on the things that unite us rather than divide us. I wanted to see people connecting more, with each other and with the planet. I wanted to stop being so unbelievably busy that I was under-valuing my relationships, experiences and surroundings. I wanted to be able to absorb the intensity of my daughter's emotions when she said 'I love you, Mum' as she drifted off to sleep, instead of feeling slightly annoyed that she still sleeps in my bed, preventing me from watching *Game of Thrones* during my only free time. I wanted to be able to watch *Game of Thrones* and bask in my daughter's love, damn it! Surely that wasn't too much to ask!

I realised that what I wanted more than anything was time, and that I could create some by disconnecting from social media. I know that a digital detox sounds like the kind of indulgence rich white women blog about while sipping on acai smoothies and having their anuses bleached, but I have found a few little tricks that have changed my relationship with my phone for the better.

1. Turn off your notifications.

You know those messages that are waiting for you every time you pick up your phone, even just to check the time or play a tune? The ones that tell you that a hundred people have texted, tweeted, Facebooked and phoned you while you were having a shower? How overwhelming are they? It's like a list of people who want something from you that never ends and you can't ignore.

Well, guess what? You can turn those off.

If that sounds uncivilised, just remember that twenty years ago we used to call people on their landline, and if they didn't answer we went and did something else for a while and then tried again later. Are you really so important that you must be contactable 24/7? Are you carrying around the world's nuclear codes? Statistically, that seems unlikely, so it's going to be okay if you get back to some people later. It's even going to be okay if you never do.

Instead, at a time of your choosing, sit down and check your messages like it's the olden days, and everything will be fine.

2. Keep it on silent. Don't even let it vibrate.
See above for benefits.

3. Delete your social media apps.

Don't panic – I'm not suggesting you delete your accounts, just your apps. You can still access them through your browser, but the experience isn't anywhere near as addictive. It's a bit clunky and irritating, which I find helps me get sick of it really quickly. It doesn't suck me in like a poker machine in the way that apps do.

17

Fix Things

BEFORE THEY'RE BADLY BROKEN

I locked myself in the chook pen again yesterday. It's the fourth time I've done it since we got the new gate, which is very high and very solid. Of course, those are exactly the qualities one looks for in a chook pen gate. It needs to keep the chickens in and the foxes out, but ideally I need to be able to choose which side of the gate I'm on.

So, yesterday morning I wandered out to feed the chickens. My children had already left to spend the day with my sister, so I was blissfully alone and planning a big day of getting things done. First on the list: feed the chooks. Out I went in my PJs, with two plastic jugs full of chickenfeed. We have four old lady chickens, who've long since ceased to lay eggs with any regularity, and if they ever do our smallest dog, who follows me into the pen, deftly steals them for his own consumption. These chickens are purely pets, and they have a lovely home, with a nice new timber fence that has a meshed window at the bottom so they don't feel cut off from the rest of the family during the day. They can see us and we can see them.

I used to let them wander around the backyard every day until sundown. Compassionate but, as usual for me, not wise, as I ended up with a yard covered in chicken poo. The little dog likes to eat chicken poo too, which is repulsive beyond words, especially as he's an affectionate little chap who likes to lick human faces. It's so hard to believe I'm still single, isn't it? You'd think men would be banging down my door for a place in this madhouse. Alas, if anyone ever does show me any interest, I assume that very fact means they're quite mad and I dismiss them immediately. As Groucho Marx once famously said, 'I don't care to belong to any club that would have me as a member.' If I ever sign up to Tinder, that will be my bio.

Anyway, yesterday there didn't seem to be any eggs in the coop. As the little dog and I were peering into the roosting box to check, we heard the metallic jangle of the gate slamming shut behind us.

'Noooo!!!' I shouted to the sky, before I even turned around. If only there'd been a drone aloft to capture the moment – it would've been quite cinematic. There we were, the little dog, the four chooks and me, trapped in the secure chicken coop of my own making.

I mentioned earlier that this was not my first time in this particular situation. On the first two occasions, my children were in the backyard and freed me quickly. The third time, they were inside watching television and I called to them for twenty minutes before one of them finally came looking for me. Last time, I called to them for so long I started wondering which of the chickens I'd eat first if push came to shove. Eventually, I realised I was in a deadset MacGyver situation and the only way out was to pit my wits against the beautifully built timber gate. I dug around in the dirt, searching for anything I could fashion into a tool. I found small toy cars, colouring pencils and a glossy magazine, before finally discovering a metal hook for hanging potted plants from ceilings. Eureka!

I twisted the hook and poked it through a small gap in the fence, painstakingly listening for evidence of contact with the metal latch. Again and again I tried to lift the latch I couldn't see. With uncharacteristic patience, I just kept at it until the gate eventually swung silently open.

Oh, Callooh Callay! I was free! Free to go inside, free to go the toilet (which I really needed to do by then), free to live my life!

And what do you think I did next? I dropped that metal hook somewhere in the garden as I strode inside, promptly forgetting all about the gate being an inescapable fortress. In fact, it was now even more so, as I had removed the only implement nearby that could open it.

This brings me to yesterday and entrapment number five. As I stood there with the little dog and the chickens, I wondered why we don't bother fixing things until they're badly broken. Why don't we seek relationship counselling until we're considering divorce? Why don't we eat better until the doctor tells us we're too fat? Why don't we streamline our lives until we feel like we're drowning?

GOOD DENIAL, AND BAD DENIAL

One of the greatest living Buddhist scholars, Lama Zopa Rinpoche, says that Buddhist centres are like spiritual emergency wards, because people who seek them out are usually in crisis. Why do we wait until things are dire before we try to make ourselves stronger? Probably for the same reasons I only think about modifying the gate when I'm trapped behind it. To function, we humans need to believe that everything is broadly fine. You only need to remember the last time you read or watched something about global warming to know how quickly we can descend into panic when confronted with the Inconvenient Truth, as it were.

Some types of denial are useful. I know there are deadly brown and tiger snakes in my neighbourhood. I must've been in close proximity to them at least a couple of times without realising it, but I don't really want to think about that. If I did, I'd never venture into the chook pen again! I'd never take my kids to the park or the beach, nor put the bins out lest I disturb one curled up behind them.

Then there's the type of denial that only causes more stress and further problems. I went through a weird phase with my children when they were three years old. On top of their father and I separating, or perhaps because of it, they started to have health issues. My son had numerous ear infections, and my daughter broke her arm, stuck a battery up her nose, and forgot she was under a table when she stood up quickly, smashing her head and giving herself whiplash. Fun times.

By the end of that year, our marriage counsellor had introduced me to the term 'hyper-vigilance'. It's an anxiety disorder that causes sufferers to become obsessed with detecting threats. Three-year-olds are pretty clumsy at the best of times, and ideally you can keep yourself from buying into the drama of it all by popping a bandaid on them, offering a cuddle and then getting on with your life. That's definitely what I do now, but when I was hyper-vigilant, the second I heard someone cry my whole body tensed, pumping with adrenalin, and I assumed I was about to be plunged into a life-changing disaster. I know it sounds over the top, and it was. I was living in a disordered emotional state. Being a single mother to three-year-old twins was definitely challenging, but I was also working through being panicked about the break-up of my marriage.

My hyper-vigilance produced so much extra tension and crazy behaviour, I felt like I was unravelling. I started to use the word 'breakdown' to describe my life. That in itself was frightening and just added to the panic even more. Around and around it went until that session with the marriage counsellor, who worked with me over the following months to help me calm down. It took a lot of counselling, meditation, reading and asking for help so that I could not only have some time for relaxation, but also properly deal with my emotions about my marriage ending. Eventually, I came back down to earth and returned to being the chilled-out, bandaid-applying, calm and cuddling mum I am today.

Denying I have a problem with the chook pen fence is stupid, because I'm going to keep getting trapped until I deal with it. Similarly, being in denial about how your unbelievable busyness is making you and your family miserable is silly. Don't put off fixing it until you're burnt out and about to collapse, or until your relationships have suffered beyond repair. By that stage, your list of problems will have grown exponentially, and your coping reserves will be correspondingly low! It's not enough to complain about being unbelievably busy – you have to actually do something about it.

18

ACCEPT

Impermanence

'Get paid to do what you love!' they tell us. The biggest problem with this rather naff advice is that what we love changes, thanks again to our old pal Impermanence. I loved meeting celebrities at first. I'd even get up a bit earlier and try to look nice for them, but that passed, probably during my first winter. Now, there isn't a celebrity in the world exciting enough to warrant my getting up earlier than I absolutely have to. Actually, I'd do it in a heartbeat for RuPaul, but no-one else.

There was a time when I loved working every hour God made, but that is not the case anymore. Now, I want naps. I suppose in theory I could get sick of naps too. I'd really like the chance to try.

Children are fantastic teachers when it comes to Impermanence. As my ex would remind me during our twins' first year, 'Everything's a phase' with kids. When my baby daughter started squealing all day long with an ear-piercing shriek, I thought she'd do me in for good, but then she stopped. That phase was over, and it was replaced by new challenges. At the moment, she's scaring the wits out of herself by thinking about zombies at bedtime. It's a nightmare trying to soothe her in the middle of the night, while controlling my fury at her father for allowing her to see a zombie-riddled computer game. (I believe him, though, when he says she begged to see it and promised she could handle it. Our daughter has always been mature and reasonable, and we've both been guilty of sometimes forgetting she's actually a child.) On the upside, she can now operate the microwave and reheat her own leftovers. She and her brother can dress themselves and are pretty self-sufficient on the toilet, so, parents of babies – don't despair! You have great changes to look forward to.

Occasionally, the knowledge that things will change has been all that's kept me going, like in the winter of 2014, when my son became prone to ear infections. This coincided with both my first separation from my husband and the biggest opportunity I'd ever had in the television industry – co-hosting a weekly, live-to-air, late-night comedy show. Before the ear infections happened, I knew my work-life balance would go out the window for a while, and I thought accepting that would help me cope until some kind of equilibrium returned. I have to admit, though, I was completely unprepared for just how unbalanced my life was about to become.

You see, approximately once a fortnight my son would wake up with an earache. 'My ear hurts, Mummy' were the dreaded words that told me that the day I'd carefully mapped out – a finely tuned spreadsheet of meetings, filming, radio and child care – was suddenly transformed into an unpredictable survival challenge. I'd need to wait at home until the local doctor's surgery opened so I could call and beg them for an appointment, then reorganise my workday (and that of all my colleagues) around whatever appointment time I could get. I'd no doubt have to extend my workday to make up the time spent at home in the morning, which meant organising extra child care, not to mention EXTENDING MY WORKDAY, which made me so tired and depressed I wanted to fake my own death and see out my days picking mangos in Darwin under an assumed name.

The thing I clung to, with increasing desperation, was the Buddhist teaching of Impermanence. While Impermanence can feel like a troubling concept when we're in a positive, happy period that we don't want to end, it can be very comforting when life is rocky. In a nutshell: good things end, which sucks, but bad things also end, which is awesome!

I don't remember when that hideous phase of my life, in which my son's ear had the power to bring a television production to its knees, ended. I don't remember the day that show ended, or the last earache, or the day we found Maria, our housekeeper who's brought so much to our lives. Sadly, we don't tend to celebrate Impermanence when it works in our favour with the same gusto we put into despising it when it turns our lives to shit.

Change can tip us off balance faster than anything. If we fail to embrace it, it can make us feel helpless, which tends to mean we either chase complete control of every situation, or pretend nothing's happening.

We all know someone whose fear of change creates obstacles in their life. Maybe they stay with a partner who's bad for them, or maybe they ignore a health problem, or maybe they're still rocking thin '90s eyebrows. Change is challenging for most of us but, for some, avoiding it is a major motivating factor in their lives. If you don't accept that life inevitably changes, whether you want it to or not, you won't be living in the real world as it actually is right now. You'll be living in a fantasy, full of delusions, and that is bound to create some very real problems in the very real world around you.

In my previous book, *Buddhism for Break-ups*, I spoke at length about how relationships can be destroyed when we refuse to accept that we and our partners have both changed. I was furious with my husband for not being the man I married almost twenty years earlier, which is crazy! I refused to deal with him as he really was, and instead wasted time and energy yearning for him as he had been in the past. When I eventually did see how he'd changed and who he'd become, I realised that though he's a great person, we just weren't romantically compatible anymore. That realisation allowed me to move through our separation and divorce in a much more positive and loving way.

A workplace, with all its monotony, can become a refuge of same-ness. Whether it's mind-numbingly boring and unful-filling, or we're hellishly overworked and undervalued, the fact that it never changes can feel very comforting in a changing world. But our unbelievable busyness can go into overdrive when we feel the need to fold in extra stuff to help us forget our job, or at least feel as though going to work isn't all we do. I have friends who take their kids to lots of extracurricular activities, I have friends who are on every school committee, and I have friends who get up before dawn to exercise. I myself have even been known to over-volunteer for great causes, and over-travel on my holidays, just to distract myself from my job. You can overdo great things just as easily as bad ones. It all comes back to balance, which is the difference between being happily busy and miserably, unbelievably busy.

As we know, we change because we're constantly being shaped by our environment (Dependent Arising). Bearing Dependent Arising in mind is a sure-fire way to improve our lives. I swear to you that you can improve your life almost instantly by making some decisions about the conditions in which you are arising. Who do you hang out with? What places and activities do you go for? What sort of entertainment do you indulge in?

If you surround yourself with competitive, superficial, judgemental people, it will be difficult to arise in any other way. If you're always with people who fetishise busyness, it will be hard to tackle your own busyness. If you and your #squad spend a lot of time bitching about people you're jealous of, you probably won't arise in a way that will help you like yourself more. Choosing to nurture positive relationships and pastimes is a big step in affecting our own arising. Choosing to entertain ourselves with positive, intelligent media will also help us grow in the right direction. Of course, there are lots of conditions about which we have little or no control, but if we control the controllable, it can have a big impact on our lives, and on how we cope when the uncontrollable comes along.

Another way to be responsible for your own arising is to tell the truth about your feelings, especially to people you trust. If you lie to look cool in front of others, you're preventing yourself from getting help, as well as giving people a false sense of who you are. How many times a day do you embellish, exaggerate or just straight out lie so someone will think better of you? How often do you play the 'Everything's Great Game' – as Nikki and Chloe did – rather than admit you're struggling? Though it might be embarrassing, think about why you do that and what it says about your self-worth.

Can we make a pact to stop doing it? Let's work on being kind, honest, open-hearted and giving – the values we should be fostering and nurturing, not busyness, or success, or popularity. Let's train ourselves to feel great about those things, no matter what else is going on in our world. That way, if we have a bad day, or take a wrong turn, or make a poor decision, or be thrown for a loop by one of life's crazy lessons, we'll still feel that there's a worthwhile part of ourselves, and that we deserve help.

19

CONFRONT HOW

Busyness

IS SERVING YOU

To hark back to our earlier discussion around addiction, I believe that when we continue with unhelpful behaviour, it must be serving us in some way, or we just wouldn't keep doing it. We must be getting something out of our unbelievable busyness, and from all the components that contribute to it, which is why we find it so hard to determine what should be deleted from our long to-do lists.

We know that our busyness hasn't just happened to us; it's the result of lots of decisions, delusions and fantasies. Therefore, we know we can beat it, but only if we figure out what we secretly love about it.

I'm sure I was the last to realise that I kind of enjoyed being a workaholic partly because it made me feel closer to my father. It felt like it was the only thing we had in common, and the only thing he's ever liked about me. I loved that my workaholism made my father think I was tough like him. So, if I changed it, we wouldn't have any connection at all.

As mentioned earlier, my unbelievable busyness also served me by being an excuse for not doing lots of things I find boring, from reading with my kids to exercising. I'm not saying I shouldn't read with my kids – on the contrary, I'm saying I should bite the bullet and do it, because ultimately it will serve me in a much more positive and long-term way, even if it takes some discipline not to defer to my 'I'm too tired' habit.

French philosopher Simone Weil said, 'Attention is the rarest and purest form of generosity.' So it stands to reason that real, focused attention on those we love is the pathway to happiness.

I had to make space not only for myself, but also for my kids. My future relationship with my children is being built right now, and their father giving up on me offered as close to a crystal ball as I was ever going to get. If I'm not careful, the day will come when my son will tell me he's too busy for me – if he ever actually accepts one of my calls.

And who would blame him? I roped everyone he knows into this terrible behaviour of justifying unbelievable busy-ness. All the other adults in his life have told him over and over that 'Mummy's busy' whenever I wasn't at an event that was important to him, or when I was late picking him up, or just unable to talk to him. We've all clearly taught him that busy people are excused many misdemeanours, and that when they finally do have time for you, it's an honour. It's sick when you see it in black and white, isn't it?

Habit is what a lot of this boiled down to. I constructed these mechanisms to help me duck and weave my way through life, and to help me overcome insecurities and past hurts. After a while it became hard to even realise there were other ways of living, let alone remember to choose them in the moment.

Feeling burdened by my family served me by making me think I was noble and unselfish. Never feeling satisfied served me by keeping me moving forward and making me feel like a high achiever. Feeling like a high achiever served my ego, and the fact that people wanted to work with me helped me feel valued. Surely it meant I was a great person, yeah?

I realised I could stop being unbelievably busy if I gave up all the reasons I secretly loved it.

I had to find the confidence to admit to my father that I'm not as tough as him, but also that there are aspects of his life I am desperate to avoid. I'm afraid of going down the same road as him physically. I don't want to work myself into a disability pension.

I had to commit to doing the boring parenting stuff that means so much to my kids. I had to find the time and mental space to give them the attention necessary for our relationship, and our mutual happiness.

I had to work on mindfulness, so that I could stop myself from blindly repeating old behaviours out of habit. I needed to develop the skills to keep checking in with myself about what I'm doing and whether there's a better way.

I had to be brave enough to be alone with myself, my thoughts and my feelings, and face whatever came up.

Unbelievable busyness served me by preventing me from thinking too deeply about my delusions and attachments. Over time, we construct our entire lives around these things, but it's tenuous, like the proverbial house of cards, and just a little introspection can bring it dangerously close to crashing down. I protected myself from that by filling my life with distractions, from work to the treats and trips it pays for. I was actually afraid of not being busy. What would I think? What would I feel? Would I cope with what was actually going on?

My new daily practice begins with setting an intention to stay mindful and present no matter how uncomfortable it feels, or how many people are yelling in my ear. A little later, when the kids are gone, I meditate instead of distracting myself, which reinforces my intention.

Meditating every day is hard to commit to. For me, it's like exercise – I never want to do it, but once I have I'm so glad I did. It helps me keep my objective of a peaceful life front of mind, and that's massive for me, because I only used to remember it at the end of every day, and it would feel like another missed opportunity. 'Why did I say yes to that?' I'd ask myself angrily, knowing I'd reflexively agreed to something that was going to take me further away from the life I wanted to live.

Now I find it easier to integrate my objectives into my decision-making. I'm able to isolate myself for a second before reacting the way I used to when an opportunity for unbelievable busyness popped up. I can remind myself that's not how I'm living anymore and move forward positively from there. It's helped me deal with all the biggies – attach-ment, fear, ego – and it really is the most powerful tool I've found in breaking destructive old habits. And, as His Holi-ness the 14th Dalai Lama says, just five minutes a day will make a difference.

20

LET GO OF THE PAST, AND

Let the Future Be

First things first: I suffer from depression. I've been on medication for it for years because it's the kind of depression that sometimes gets hold of me and won't let go. At its worst, it spirals into complete despondency and I can't see any point in being alive. That's when I know it's time to talk to my doctor about adjusting my medication.

I know that's full-on, but I want to be honest about it so you don't get the impression that I think meditation and incense are enough to get you through mental health issues. I have no doubt that Buddha would recommend utilising any and all medical and professional help at our disposal, but that he would also advise us to participate in our treatment as much as possible. It's not enough to ask others to 'fix' us; we must give ourselves every chance at healing.

Let's revisit my favourite saying: 'When I'm depressed, I'm living in the past. When I'm anxious, I'm living in the future.'

Brain chemistry seizes on future- and past-thinking to varying degrees. Some people can work their way out of both and back into the present pretty easily, while some of us require a bit of pharmaceutical assistance. Unlike the illicit drugs I used to rely on to help me cope, my anti-depressants don't distort my reality, or send me crashing back down to earth eventually, or make me think I'm being really funny when I'm just being mean. I can still feel depressed while taking anti-depressants, but it stays at a manageable level at which I can apply logical, self-soothing techniques.

My depression usually grows out of regret and embarrassment over something I've said or done. I go over and over it in my mind, as though remembering it will somehow enable me to go back and change it. My depression lives on self-flagellation. I was raised Catholic, after all!

My ex-husband now admits to suffering from depression in the last years of our marriage. He says it was because his life wasn't what he wanted it to be, and he didn't know what to do about it. He doesn't use the words embarrassment or regret, though. He uses a much tougher word: shame.

It's hard to admit to being embarrassed, because it's embarrassing all over again. We usually try to fob it off by pretending we meant to act that way all along. Shame is even harder to own, isn't it? It describes a very deep feeling of unworthiness and lack of compassion for oneself.

For all sorts of minor infractions, my mother used to say, 'You should be thoroughly ashamed of yourself.' It became water off a duck's back to me, and I certainly didn't feel ashamed about my untidy room or being rude to my sister. Her overuse of the word made it meaningless until, as an adult seeking enlightenment, I began investigating my emotions and discovered I actually was thoroughly ashamed of myself for all sorts of reasons, some reasonable and some downright ridiculous.

I'm a very clumsy person, both physically and verbally. If there's a glass to knock over, I'll find it; if there's an awkward question to be asked in a social situation, I'll find that too, and then spill my wine all over you as punctuation.

I'm the kind of person who asks, 'How's that fabulous wife of yours?' when, of course, she's left him. 'How's the business going?' Of course, it's in liquidation. 'How's your lovely dog?' Inevitably, it died that day, and the children, who are present, don't know yet. I'm a menace to society and shouldn't be let out.

I remember telling my friend Toby many years ago, after some social indiscretion or other, that I wished I was a ventriloquist's dummy, locked away in a suitcase under a bed until it was time to perform my act, and then put safely back in there after a good antiseptic wipedown. On stage, I'm razor-sharp; socially, I'm an idiot.

I've become slightly better with age. I've learnt to stop asking questions about people and pets who aren't in the room, and I always avoid contentious topics of conversation, even if the lay of the land is exposed and brightly lit. It seems there's more to disagree about than ever these days, and I've trained myself not to flinch when a seemingly reasonable person tries to tell me that some fascist moron in the news 'actually has some good ideas'.

But just when I think I'm impervious to social stuff-ups, I invariably come unstuck, and begin the process of replaying the incident repeatedly and obsessing over what I should've said or done. This, of course, takes me out of the present, and I become consumed by disturbing emotions of anger, regret and shame.

Again, mindfulness through meditation can help break this old pattern by enabling me to calmly observe my thoughts and emotions, in order to approach them logically and intellectually. As we know, it's useful to intellectualise our way out of emotional confusion. In fact, it's the only way out. As the Buddhist teacher Nagarjuna put it:

If there is a remedy when trouble strikes,
what reason is there for despondency?
And if there is no help for it,
What is the use of being sad?

He was telling us that there are only two logical ways to deal with a problem. If there's a solution to the problem, then we need not feel dejected; we just need to get on with that solution. If there's no solution, then what's the use of being sad? It's a waste of time and energy that could be spent on something positive and productive.

LET THE FUTURE BE

When I'm anxious, I'm living in the future.

We know that you can't live peacefully if you're always focused on the future, yet for so long I was convinced I couldn't experience peace unless I'd made certain provisions for the future. It's important not to forget to apply some wisdom here. Remember, we aren't talking about ignoring the future in a hedonistic way; we're talking about not 'living' in the future to the extent that you're missing the present. Do those sensible things that will help your future self survive – make sure there's milk for tomorrow morning, save a few bucks every month, wear sunscreen – but don't deny yourself happiness, peace and good health today because you're banking on it paying off later.

It's time to look at the final two of Buddha's Four Noble Truths. Here's a wonderful interpretation I found online of all four truths:

1. Suffering happens all the time because people always want more or something better than what we have.
2. Because we don't have what we want, we suffer and feel upset.

3. If we accept what we have and stop wanting more, we will become happy.

4. Following the Noble Eightfold Path will help achieve this.

We can see how the first two noble truths are tied to future-thinking. They're all about wanting things we don't have, wanting our future – whether five minutes or five years from now – to be 'better', and suffering because we can't be happy in the present moment.

The third noble truth is about engaging with the present reality, and being grateful for what you already have. You've already started this by doing the self-reflection exercise at the end of Chapter 3. Now, it's time to step it up and make it one of your daily intentions. Say to yourself every morning, 'My intention today is to be grateful for what I have in my life.' Setting your intention to appreciate today while giving yourself the best possible opportunity for a better tomorrow will help you cope with difficulties as they arise. You will realise they are temporary, and generally outnumbered by good bits. In order for this to work properly, though, you have to begin with your gratitude bar really low. Start with being grateful for waking up this morning, because not everyone did. Be grateful for whatever food and drink you have for breakfast, because not everybody can afford to eat today. And be grateful for the freedom with which you move about the world, because not everyone is as free. It's all about perspective.

THE EIGHTFOLD PATH

The fourth noble truth says you can engage with the present and find greater happiness by following the Eightfold Path. It's essentially Buddha's suggested checklist for life, so let's look at it now.

1. Right View

Seeing life as it really is. Doing away with delusions and projections, distractions and avoidance mechanisms and seeking the truth in every situation, no matter how unpleasant or inconvenient it is. It also means seeing and accepting Impermanence in everything.

2. Right Intentions

Always being motivated by generosity, love and compassion. Intention is everything in Buddhism. *Why* you do something is much more significant than the action itself. It reminds me of one of my favourite stories from my Catholic childhood. Jesus once sat observing people giving donations at the temple. He watched as several wealthy men made a big show of adding serious amounts of cash to the total, but he was most impressed with the offering of one particular woman.

> Then one poor widow came and put in two small copper coins, which amounted to a small fraction of a denarius. Jesus called His disciples to Him and said, 'Truly I tell you, this poor widow has put more than all the others into the treasury. For they all contributed out of their surplus, but she out of her poverty has put in all she had to live on.'
>
> MARK 12:42-44

What was the intention behind the men's donations, and what was the intention behind the woman's? I think Buddha would've enjoyed Jesus's observation here.

I'm not opposed to public acts of generosity, because I believe they encourage others to be generous. If your intention is to raise awareness of a cause by telling others of your commitment to it, then I think that qualifies as right intention. But if your intention is to look like a great, successful person who should be applauded – well, that's not so good. The truth is, most of us fall somewhere in between, but hopefully we err on the side of right intention.

This isn't just about big acts of generosity, though. Ideally, right intentions should be part of our day-to-day existence. If we get out of bed with the intention of treating our family with patience and kindness, that's right intention. If we get into our car with the intention of behaving reasonably in traffic, that's right intention. If we walk into work with the intention of doing our best and treating our colleagues with compassion, that's right intention.

Setting our intention is an example of wise future-thinking. It's not about getting something or someone else to make us happy. It's about acknowledging that I am the only person who can make me happy, and I'm the only person who can make me the person I want to be.

3. Right Speech

This is about communicating truthfully, respectfully and positively.

I used to work with a friend called Sonia, whose classic saying was, 'Nah, mate, fuck that!' I consider that to be right speech because whenever she said it, she was being absolutely truthful and unequivocal about her belief that something was a bad idea. It always made everyone on the team laugh, so it created a great environment in which to exchange honest opinions.

I'm aware that people in other environments found it a bit hurtful and intimidating. Right speech requires wisdom and compassion, like everything else, because what determines its rightness is its impact on others. Increasingly, language and how it affects people is regarded as a serious matter in public spaces, especially online.

While I've always thought of myself as respectful, I used to say things on stage and even on radio that I wouldn't say now. Standards change, and we need to change with them. I'd hate to hurt someone's feelings with my words, particularly if it was a throwaway comment without real meaning.

I once had a conversation with an AM radio shock jock in which he joked about stirring up his listeners about Muslim women wearing burqas. I so wish I could tell you his name, believe me, because he made it very clear that he doesn't really care about the issue, but he falls back on it when he needs people to call his radio show and nothing else he's talking about is getting them going. That sort of stirring leads to the abuse and assault of innocent women and girls in Australia. The fact that he believes it's silly, and knows it motivates others to deeper hatred, is clearly not right speech. It's also an example of bad intentions. It's just a karmic disaster all round, really, but it's the kind of stuff many people indulge in on their social media platforms.

There are many 'likes' to be had in certain circles by sharing inflammatory rhetoric. The truth and origins of the material are often dubious, but it raises attention for the poster, and that feels nice for them. The fact that it feels horrible for people whose lives are lived in the shadow of bigotry gets lost in the entertainment value of watching it blow up.

We've all seen the 'concerned mum' posts about issues like sex ed in schools, which are really nothing more than alarmist rumour sharing. I've debunked several on my own Facebook page, only to see them continue to spread like wildfire. It seems that users think something must be true because they've seen it shared a lot, and 'where there's smoke, there's fire'.

Please remember that's not the case. Where there's smoke, there's just a lot of bored people with nothing better to do than fan the flames.

In fact, just like in the old days before social media, the things that get shared the most are the juiciest rumours. I'm sure you can remember a time when you believed a stupid rumour because everyone was talking about it. It's incumbent upon all of us in this incredibly connected world to take responsibility for what we contribute. Social media has made right speech more important than ever, because our speech can travel so far now. Think about that next time you post or share. Are you sure about the truth and helpfulness of what you're sharing? Is your post going to hurt anyone?

It's embarrassing to realise you still say something that's now deemed offensive, especially if you still find it funny. I've been there. I've had a guilty laugh at the memory of jokes that would now ignite a scandal if they were aired in public, but we can't engage destructive emotions to cover up our embarrassment, leading us to lash out at those hurt by our language.

It's rather amazing that Buddha's idea of using language carefully and kindly has been around for two and a half thousand years, long before the invention of Twitter!

4. Right Action

This one encompasses the five precepts, the basic code of ethical conduct taught by Buddha: don't steal, don't kill, don't lie, don't indulge in sexual misconduct, and don't take drugs or other intoxicants. It's beneficial to look deeply into our behaviour and be honest about the many ways in which we are breaking those simple rules every day.

Ignoring environmental challenges and continuing our lives of high consumption steals clean air and water from future generations. Betcha didn't think about that, did ya! Eating meat makes us complicit in the killing of animals (again, for our big old consumption party), and pretending we don't realise all of that is overburdening the planet is lying. Using sex to manipulate and control others is sexual misconduct, so remember that next time you promise someone a little bedtime favour if they unstack the dishwasher or bath the kids.

I'm not feeling particularly superior now, by the way – I've broken all these rules today! I'm just trying to keep us all mindful of the impact our actions have on each other and the world around us. Remember, Buddha realised we are all connected, and everything we do affects everyone else. While it would be virtually impossible for most of us to refrain completely from breaking these rules, it's good for us to stay honest about our imperfections at least.

5. Right Livelihood

In other words, make a living that is not at the expense of others. Buddha promoted the principle of equality for all living things and respect for all life. If your income creates suffering for others then you're not kicking goals as far as Buddhism is concerned. I get that beggars can't be choosers, and I also get that with our interconnected economy it seems like everyone's getting shafted in one way or another, but it's important that we try, with everything we've got, to make a living without hurting anyone else.

As I mentioned earlier, I was a brothel receptionist for a while in the '90s. The places were clean and legal, and the women definitely chose to work there, but there were times when I coaxed them to stay longer, or to come in on their days off, so that I could keep the door open and earn more money. Looking back, I'd have to say I was not always making a right livelihood in those days.

6. Right Effort

Having an open mind and a balanced approach to life and work. This requires positive thinking backed up by focused action, but also an understanding of the importance of rest and contemplation!

7. Right Mindfulness

Being aware of the moment you are in and focusing on it. Thinking about neither the future nor the past – only the present. It isn't about shutting out the world, but rather being right there in it and truly engaging with it.

8. Right Concentration

This is about pursuing a level of mental discipline that will allow you to meditate effectively and productively. It is through this that one can achieve right mindfulness and right effort.

21

BE GRATEFUL FOR THE

Little Things

When I started thinking about writing this book, I happened to be running away from my life in very auspicious surroundings. I was in Bodhgaya, India, the place in which Buddha meditated under the Bodhi tree until he reached enlightenment some two and a half thousand years ago. It's Buddhist ground zero.

Not only that, the town of around 40,000 people was hosting upwards of 250,000 Buddhist visitors, including His Holiness the 14th Dalai Lama and his most trusted advisers (and Richard Gere!). We were all there for an event called the Kalachakra, a fairly intense gathering that lasts for two weeks.

The low, hypnotic chanting of Tibetan monks blared from speakers in the streets day and night. Robed monks and nuns seemed to outnumber laypeople, and old Tibetans and Bhutanese, with faces so carved by the elements they looked like relief maps of the Himalayas, mumbled mantras while rolling smooth prayer beads between their knotted fingers. It was intense and overwhelming, and I suspected I only understood about 50 per cent of what was going on. But it was wonderful. I was in heaven.

Visiting India, and this place in particular, had been a dream of mine since I really started studying Buddhism seriously in 2007. I began IVF in 2008, which took care of any excess cash, and ever since the twins were born, I've weighed up how and when I could manage this trip. Should I wait until they're old enough to come with me? How old would that be? It seemed insane for so many reasons. But, as the old Chinese proverb says, 'When the student is ready, the teacher appears,' and my teacher materialised in the form of a stranger at Brisbane airport.

This kind lady approached me to say that she loved the Dalai Lama (because she knew I did) and to ask if I'd ever been to one of his big teachings in India. I told her I hadn't, but was always thinking about it. I said that my small children made it difficult for me to go. 'Should I take them?' I asked her.

'Oh, Christ no!' she exclaimed, startling everyone in the departure lounge. 'Not unless you want to sit on a packed Indian train for ten hours with two gastro-ridden kids!'

'No,' I answered, 'I most certainly do not want to do that.'

'I've got kids around the same age as yours,' she continued. 'When I went to India, I just told them that visiting His Holiness was going to make me a better mum, and you know what? It really did.'

Well, that got me thinking. I'd always thought that going without my kids would be incredibly selfish, but I could see the logic in what my new friend was telling me. 'Remember,' she yelled after me as I left for my flight, 'you have to be the best person you can be, if you want to be their best mum!'

That conversation changed things for me. As I sat on my flight back to Melbourne, I thought a lot about the kind of human being I was, and the kind I wanted to be. I had to concede there was a widening gap between the two.

Four years later, with the gap wider than ever, I finally made it to India. And like the complete cliché I am, the trip was life-changing. I really did gain a new and fascinating perspective on my own existence. It's hard not to, as you wander the dusty, chaotic streets with tiny, bedraggled children pulling at your clothes with one hand and miming their need for food with the other. It made me more aware of the luckiness of my life than ever before. I mean, I try to be aware of it all the time, and I pester my kids endlessly about it, but India made me *know* it in every molecule of my body and every electrical spark in my brain. I was born to my circumstances in Australia, and those children in India were born to theirs. Neither of us deserved it; it's just the luck of the draw. Though our place of birth doesn't completely define our life, clearly we can be born into great advantage or great disadvantage. With blinding clarity, I realised the good fortune with which I've been #blessed.

I'm not rich or beautiful, and I've never won the lottery, but without a doubt I am lucky. On top of my lucky birth, I have a healthy body and mind, and a loving family. For a long time, though, I disrespected that good fortune by focusing on what I didn't have.

In India, aspects of my life suddenly seemed really stupid. (I was also wearing socks with sandals, so my decision-making certainly took an unexpected turn.)

I couldn't see the point anymore of my endless rushing around, never feeling satisfied, and the long hours I spent away from my kids. In a way, even the fact that I was in India pointed to the lack of balance in my life, as I'd booked the expensive trip in a moment of frustration about not being able to concentrate on Buddhism as much as I'd like to. I was always trying to get to my local Buddhist centre, the Tara Institute in Melbourne, but I never had the time or energy to make the hour-long trip across town.

After only a few days, the fog of confusion over my life lifted, which is rather ironic because the air there was as brown as weak tea. Visibility was so bad one day that I thought I saw a fully grown cow browsing the cigarette counter inside the local shop. As I got closer, I realised she was actually browsing the biscuits. The owner opened a packet of butter tea biscuits and fed them to the cow two at a time, without so much as a smile let alone a baby-voiced pretend conversation. There's just no way I could feed tea biscuits to a cow inside a shop without a baby-voiced pretend conversation about how clever the cow is, how much she likes biscuits and what plans she might have for the rest of the day. Old-mate shopkeeper, though, seemed to see nothing even faintly adorable about the situation, and when I tried to get a photo they both gave me side eye, as if every steak I'd ever eaten was written all over my face, before telepathically agreeing to ignore me.

A small girl grabbed my arm and led me to a blanket shop. Without speaking English, she made it clear that I was to buy her and her family a big blanket, upon which they would all live, as they'd outgrown their old one. It was as if every nice blanket I'd ever owned was written all over my face, too, so I paid up and she skipped off with the blanket without a backward glance. I reckon the cow would have a better chance of picking me out of a line-up than that kid.

That night, as I sat on my itchy bed, I thought about that girl, and about all the children living on blankets on dusty streets. The world is sometimes not good and wise, as King Suchandra so rightly pointed out, but Buddha helped him realise that the task wasn't to change the world, the task was to change himself.

A quote from Mother Teresa popped into my mind:

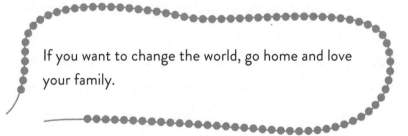

If you want to change the world, go home and love your family.

So, that's what I did.

Lots of things have changed in the year or so since I came home from India. I've given up my high-paying but thoroughly exhausting job, for one thing, which is terrifying and exhilarating all at once.

For the first time in fifteen years I'm not trying to work my way up my industry. I'm not chasing more. I'm actually trying to float gently down to a place of just enough. Just enough work to keep me creatively fulfilled but not absorbed in it, at the expense of the rest of my life. Just enough money to keep us fed and warm (with the odd treat thrown in, of course!). Just enough time to sit quietly with myself, and just enough time to spend really engaged with others.

I'm not sure how I'm going to go with that, to tell you the truth. I suspect it's going to take a lot of discipline to be able to feel the fear and stay the course anyway. I set my intention every morning when I wake, and I remain mindful as I prepare my kids for school, which I've never been around to do before. I suck in the joy of those moments.

When they're gone and the house is silent, I meditate and listen to all my fears about the changes I've made in my life. One by one I acknowledge them, and then send them away so I can get back to listening to my breath, my life force, and reflecting on the joy of living to see another day.

This way of living feels better for me, now. It wouldn't have ten years ago, and it may not ten years from now, but in this moment it feels right, and this is the only moment I can live in.

I hope you can dig deep enough inside yourself to figure out what's right for you in this moment. Be kind to yourself, practise mindfulness and remember always the middle path, no extremes. We're not aiming for perfection or cinematic journeys – this isn't *MasterChef*! We're just trying to get down to what's real and true and good inside of us. We're being the human beings we want to be.

Good luck.